A Threefold Cord

A SINGLE MOTHER'S JOURNEY OF FAITH

AZARIAH NASYA

TRILLIUM SAGE

Book Cover by GetCovers

Illustrations by Azariah Nasya

Edited by N. Chow

ISBNs:

979-8-9905613-0-4 | ebook

979-8-9905613-1-1 | paperback

979-8-9905613-2-8 | hardcover

I dedicate this book to anyone who has suffered or is currently suffering from abuse of any kind. I can personally tell you that the LORD hears your cries for help, and He will take care of you if you place your trust in Him.

Give your burdens to the LORD, and He will take care of you.
He will not permit the godly to slip and fall.
Psalm 55:22 NLT

A Threefold Cord

Introduction

Although I have had a brief life of 43 years thus far, it has become quite fulfilling from the moment I invited Jesus into my heart. In the midst of trial, we often do not have an accurate perspective–especially when the threefold cord is not complete within us. By "threefold cord," of course, I am referring to the Scripture in Ecclesiastes 4:12 KJV, which says: *And if one prevails against him, two shall withstand him; and a threefold cord is not quickly broken.*

This Scripture is a popular verse for couples in marriage; however, it can also refer to our relationship with the Trinity (The Father, Son, and Holy Spirit). It also could refer to a special relationship with a mother, grandmother, father, grandfather, or–well, you get the picture. There is much wisdom gained from difficulty, trial, mistakes, and suffering–mainly because there is a lesson that God wants us to learn through them.

The world tells us that tears and humility are for the weak, but as we read and study God's Word of Truth, we soon discover those are lies of the enemy. When you grow up in such dysfunction as I did, without a solid foundation, it is easy for those lies to become believable. James 1:2-4 ESV says: *Count it all joy, my brothers, when you meet trials of various kinds, for you know that the testing of your faith produces steadfastness. And let steadfastness have its full effect, that you may be perfect and complete, lacking in nothing.* When I first read this verse, I thought this was completely impossible to accomplish and was not sure that this was entirely accurate. Now that my eyes are more open to the Word of Truth, I treasure this Scripture and am able to thank God in the midst of hardship. I hope that you are blessed by my story, and if you are in the middle of a storm, remember that you never walk alone.

Chapter One

MY BEGINNING

I was born approximately one month prematurely and weighed just over five pounds. I was born to a mother who had borne a son a year and a half before conceiving me, and she strongly opposed another child. My father, meanwhile, desperately wanted two children—one boy and one girl. I later learned from my paternal grandmother Ruthie (who was the one genuine, loving, believing family member in my life) that my father won the argument between my mother and him through deception by telling her that he would wear protection. He did not.

Looking back on my childhood, I remember a lot of yelling and not much love or affection shown toward one another. My father is Italian and grew up in a very strict Catholic home with six sisters. He was a workaholic, and I barely saw him. When I did, he was drinking alcohol, smoking marijuana, and yelling at my mother. My mother is of Eastern European and Indian descent. She grew up in an abusive and incestual home, and was baptized Lutheran. Her family had a history of mental illness; her brother (my uncle) was gay and had bipolar disorder, and her oldest sister (my aunt) had schizophrenia. She also worked a lot and spent a lot of time away from home. So, my brother and I were often left home alone, and I learned how to take care of my brother and me.

When my father and my mother forsake me,
then the LORD will take me up.
Psalm 27:10 KJV

My paternal grandmother, Ruthie, a truly genuine and caring presence in my life, invested time and effort in creating memorable experiences with me during my early years. When I was four, Ruthie adorned me with water wings and introduced me to the backyard pool at her and my grandfather's house. Though initially fearful, I gradually adapted and found joy in the experience. As I turned five, my grandmother took the initiative to enroll me in swimming lessons, faithfully accompanying me every week. I am deeply grateful for her involvement, which played a pivotal role in helping me learn the valuable skill of swimming.

In contrast, my maternal grandparents exhibited a dysfunctional dynamic and frequently showed reluctance to spend time with my brother and me. Despite my mother's attempts to drop us off at their house under the guise of "running errands," the connection between us and our maternal grandparents remained strained. At age eight, I found myself alone at my maternal grandparents' house when my mother dropped me off and my brother was at a friend's place. Fortunately, my eldest aunt resided with them, and my cousin provided company for me during that time.

While we were playing in the yard on a hot day, my maternal grandfather offered to dish us both some ice cream. This was a lure to get both of us girls inside the house. When we got inside, he did not get us ice cream. Instead, he told us both to wait on the couch while he got our ice cream. He came back empty-handed and approached us both with his pants off.

My cousin and I both ran to get away from him and hid in a closet, but he found us, stripped our clothes off, and had his way with us. My maternal grandmother and my aunt were inside the house while this was happening. They heard our screams, but nobody in the house did anything at all.

I sensed a chill creeping over me, an uneasy blend of fear and vulnerability. Without hesitation, I slipped through the shadows of the back door and darted away, covering three blocks to the south until I reached the comforting haven of my paternal grandparents' home. It was my paternal grandmother who, with a phone call, alerted my mother and summoned the authorities to the unfolding situation. Strangely absent from the investigation was any scrutiny directed toward my maternal grandfather, a detail that I only realized later. In an unsettling turn, my mother, against my instincts, attempted to coax me back into that unsettling environment; she asked me to return to my maternal grandparents' house. It was only the firm resolve of my paternal grandmother that demanded my presence at her house, a refuge from the storm that threatened to engulf me.

In the sanctuary of my paternal grandmother's home, she unfolded revelations with a voice steeped in compassion. Her words resonated with a constant prayer for me, a prayer that she believed had divine echoes, a prayer affirming my uniqueness. She spoke of an impending journey through hardships, but assured me that blessings, akin to those bestowed upon exceptional women, awaited me. Comparing my heart to that of Mother Teresa, she envisioned a path where I would extend aid to those in need.

Amidst this revelation, she unraveled a tapestry of truths concealed by my mother's deceit. Contrary to the narrative my mother presented to me, my brother had been fed a tale of equal love and desire for both of us. The dissonance between my mother's aversion towards me and her affirmations to my brother left me perplexed.

In a transformative moment, my paternal grandmother guided me through a visual journey, presenting photographs capturing my mother's fragility before my birth. The images portrayed a thin figure, taken when she was seven months pregnant with me. It became evident that my mother's nutritional deprivation during pregnancy was a cause for concern. My grandmother, who had persistently encouraged my mother to eat, disclosed the stark contrast between the falsehoods my mother propagated and the harsh reality she faced. Armed with this newfound clarity, I began to navigate the complex landscape of truth and falsehoods woven into my past, anchored by the unwavering support of Ruthie.

> *"Then you will know the truth,*
> *and the truth will set you free."*
> **John 8:32 NIV**

In the aftermath of that incident, my mother's response was to leave my brother and me alone at home, imposing a strict rule that confined us within the house. This marked the beginning of a period of solitude and isolation that defined much of my childhood. Left to my own devices, I found solace in a world of imagination, crafting scenarios where I belonged to a warm and loving family.

Throughout my upbringing, there were numerous instances where I felt divinely shielded from the malevolence surrounding me. A pivotal intervention came in the form of my paternal grandmother, an instrument of God's protection. She played a crucial role in preventing me from returning to the tumultuous environment of my maternal grandparents' home, serving as a safeguard in the midst of chaos.

> *For He will command His angels concerning you*
> *to guard you in all your ways.*
> **Psalm 91:11 NIV**

I was a very curious and adventurous girl growing up. I always wanted to be a teacher when I got older. I was mostly quiet, unless spoken to. I observed a lot in silence and spoke very little unless there was an injustice of some sort happening around me or if I was learning something. I would ask a lot of questions.

My tomboyish nature led me outdoors, where I reveled in unstructured play. The earth beneath my feet became a canvas for exploration—dirt, mud, grass, and water were my companions. Among all these, the towering trees held a special place in my heart, providing a sense of security that eluded me within the walls of my home. One particular crabapple tree, nestled in the corner of our garden, became my sanctuary. God made its upper branches the perfect refuge, my makeshift "fort" offering an escape from the dysfunction that permeated my home and the tumultuous atmosphere surrounding my mother's family. I spent many hours in that tree, and I was always at peace there.

This tree was a testament to God's miraculous presence in a moment of intervention. It was a formidable challenge, but one day, my determined spirit urged me to conquer it. As I ascended, pushing myself to the limit, I found myself just two or three branches away from the pinnacle.

Then came the unexpected. The branch beneath my foot gave way, and I plummeted from a considerable height. The ground rushed up to meet me, and at the tree's base lay a familiar picnic bench, a spot where we often shared family lunches. In that heart-stopping descent, my head collided with both the table and the bench. Given the height of the fall, the impact, and my tender age, the potential for broken bones seemed imminent.

Yet, miraculously, not a bone was shattered, nor was there a single scratch on my body. Despite a momentary experience of pain, the divine intervention was palpable. I emerged unscathed from what could have easily resulted in severe injury, a testament to God watching over me in that precarious moment.

At the age of 10, I found myself in another precarious situation, this time within the confines of an old three-story barn near my friend's house. The barn resonated with the echoes of our playful laughter as we explored the aged structure. My friend, fueled by youthful daring, raced to the summit using a weathered ladder that ascended to the barn's third story. From her elevated perch, she beckoned me to join her at the top. In the carefree spirit of childhood and extending into adolescence and early adulthood, my nature was marked by impulsivity and a tendency to act without pondering the potential consequences.

In a heartbeat, I accepted the challenge, racing up the ladder with an almost instant determination. However, God had other plans. Just three steps from the pinnacle, the wooden step beneath me splintered, sending me into a free fall from the barn's third story. The dirt floor awaited me below, featuring an unforgiving rock right beneath the ladder. My descent concluded with a direct impact on my tailbone against the unyielding surface.

The initial sensation was sharp, the pain welling up momentarily as tears threatened to spill from my eyes. Yet, almost as swiftly as the pain had arrived, it vanished completely. Despite the significant fall and the direct impact on a solid rock, there were no discernible signs of injury. An obligatory visit to the hospital ensued, but medical examinations revealed no traces of harm. Such instances, scattered throughout my life, remain etched in my memory. It's a tapestry of moments where divine protection seems the only plausible explanation. In reflection, I am left with an overwhelming sense that only God could have orchestrated such interventions, providing a shield of safeguard in the face of potential harm.

> *I will say of the LORD,*
> *"He is my refuge and my fortress,*
> *My God in whom I trust*
> *(with great confidence, and on whom I rely)!"*
> **Psalm 91:2 AMP**

Chapter Two

SEARCHING

I have always been searching for love, belonging, purpose, identity, independence, and validation–in childhood, mostly, but I have always longed for these things. Even now, some may be able to relate to this feeling.

At the tender age of 11, a day unfolded with a sense of unease, a visceral feeling in my gut signaling an impending sense of doom. On that particular day, my mother had begun preparing dinner, the aroma of simmering pasta wafting through the air. Engrossed in a book, I rose from my room to heed the call of nature, only to be met with an acrid scent and the ominous sight of smoke billowing from the stove. The shrill wail of the smoke detector punctuated the air.

Swiftly, I removed the pan from the stove, quelling the source of the smoke, and turned off the burner. My immediate concern turned to locating my mother, but she was conspicuously absent. A thorough search of our home, spanning both front and back yards, yielded no trace of her. Fueled by worry, I expanded my search to the neighbor's house, a place she frequented.

I knocked loudly on the neighbor's front door, and there was no answer. So, I walked inside and heard voices coming from the bedroom. I walked around the corner to see my mother and the neighbor both naked and having intercourse. I screamed and ran back home. That was how I discovered my mother's infidelity to my father.

I remember being somewhat traumatized by seeing that, and when I had the opportunity, I told my father what I had seen. In the dim glow of my bedroom, the voices of my parents arguing clashed like distant thunder, reverberating through the paper-thin walls. Seeking solace from the nightly storm, I nestled under my covers, cocooned in silence beneath the comforting weight of a pillow pressed firmly against my ears.

As I stepped into adolescence, the weariness stemming from my parents' ceaseless arguments and the palpable tension within our home became too much to bear. Seeking solace, I turned to my teachers and school friends, sharing the tumultuous details of my home life. Compassionate parents of some friends offered me refuge, assuring me that their homes were open whenever I needed an escape. It was at the age of 11, under the weight of familial discord, that I embarked on my first attempt to break free. The restricting and uncomfortable tension of home life drove me on a quest for identity and independence.

One late afternoon, around 5 pm, I set out on foot, a young wanderer seeking refuge from the storm of domestic strife. As I walked down the road, my senses heightened, I encountered a pickup truck brimming with teenagers. Some faces were familiar, and as the truck slowed down beside me, a voice from the back called out, "Hey, do you need a ride?" Despite a nagging sense of unease, I chose to bury my reservations and climbed into the bed of the truck.

> *But I am afraid that just as*
> *Eve was deceived by the serpent's cunning,*
> *your minds may somehow be led astray*
> *from your sincere and pure devotion to Christ.*
> **2 Corinthians 11:3 NIV**

In the truck, I made the decision not to face my solitude, opting instead for the company of the teenage boy behind the wheel. As fate would have it, the gravel road became treacherous, and the truck skidded off into a thicket. The collision catapulted me from the truck bed, where I collided with a tree, the impact reverberating through my head and shoulder. Consciousness faded, replaced by the distant murmur of someone inquiring about my well-being. When awareness returned, I found myself in the sterile surroundings of a hospital room.

My father, summoned by someone, stood by my side, and I was eventually driven back home. The examining doctor relayed that while I had been briefly unconscious due to the force of the impact, no apparent damage was evident. It was a moment of disobedience on my part, a deviation from the path I should have chosen. Yet, despite my actions, a divine grace seemed to shield me from harm. In hindsight, this should have been a clear revelation of God's protective hand in my life. However, my vision was clouded by the complexities of my circumstances, preventing me from fully grasping the gravity of Ruthie's words and prayers for me.

None is righteous, no, not one;
Romans 3:10 ESV

A thousand may fall at your side
and ten thousand at your right hand,
but danger will not come near you.
Psalm 91:7 AMP

In moments of distress, I often sought solace in the presence of those around me, seeking physical comfort instead of turning to the One who remains steadfast. Despite the challenges, not every aspect of my life during this period was marred by negativity. A vivid memory from when I was 12 stands out–a camping trip with my paternal grandparents.

Before delving into this recollection, it's essential to understand my paternal grandfather's background. Hailing from Italy, his upbringing was marred by adversity, marked by an abusive father entrenched in the world of the Italian mafia. His demeanor reflected the shadows of a tumultuous past; he was a moody figure prone to outbursts directed at my grandmother, his children, myself, and the other grandchildren.

During that camping excursion, my paternal grandparents generously gathered all seven grandchildren for the adventure. My youngest cousin and I were allocated the camper, sharing sleeping quarters with our grandmother, while the older cousins set up camp in a sizable tent just outside with our grandfather. Much of my time was spent in the company of my grandmother, assisting in meal preparations and attending to the needs of my grandfather. However, amid the harmonious moments, there were instances of discord. One vivid memory involves my grandfather's return from a hunting expedition. I was engaged in playful activities outside the camper, and a persistent bee triggered my fear, prompting a terrified scream. In response, my grandfather rebuked me, branding me a coward and insisting I dispatch the intruding bee. This encounter was followed by an unconventional "bath" in the frigid creek—an unforgettable experience, to say the least.

Despite challenging moments like these, the camping trip remained a positive experience. The credit goes to my paternal grandmother, who skillfully ensured that her grandchildren felt cherished and esteemed, even in the face of our grandfather's tumultuous behavior. Nurturing a collection of cherished moments with my paternal grandmother became a wellspring of hope for me. In those instances of joy and connection, even when the broader landscape seemed bleak, I clung to a steadfast and confident hope for the future. Amid unseen challenges, my prayers to God became a constant plea for His guidance and assistance.

Rejoice in our confident hope.
Be patient in trouble and keep on praying.
Romans 12:12 NLT

Look to the LORD and His strength;
seek His face always.
Psalm 105:4 NIV

Recollections of rare overnight stays with friends and their families stand out as treasured memories from my adolescence. One particular friend from middle school, whom I'll refer to as Heather, became a source of comfort. Despite her parents being separated, Heather's home emanated genuine love. In the nurturing environment, even after the school bell rang, I found solace in her mother's warm embrace. Heather's mother, despite the circumstances, went above and beyond to create lasting memories. From shared ice cream outings to movie nights, she seamlessly wove a tapestry of love and joy. Dress-up sessions added an extra layer of warmth, making her home a haven of affection.

Another friend, Emily, provided a different yet equally enriching experience. Hailing from a large Mormon family, their values centered around togetherness. In their company, I felt not only welcomed but embraced as an honorary family member. These moments, intertwined with the warmth of my paternal grandmother's love, remain etched in my mind as some of the most memorable and pleasant chapters of my youth.

During those times of shared warmth and genuine connections, my faith in God played a pivotal role in cultivating a confident hope. As I experienced love within the homes of friends and their families, a conviction grew within me that such genuine affection was attainable for myself one day. In the embrace of those moments, I found solace in the belief that God's plan held the promise of encompassing such love and connection in my own life.

This hope (this confident assurance) we have
as an anchor of the soul
(it cannot slip and it cannot break down under whatever pressure bears
upon it)—
a safe and steadfast hope that enters within the veil
(of the heavenly temple,
that most Holy Place
in which the very presence of God dwells).
Hebrews 6:19 AMP

Chapter Three

DYSFUNCTION

At the adolescent age of 14, my home life began to unravel, giving way to a tumultuous environment. The strains in my parents' marriage, already palpable, escalated into more intense and frequent arguments. Concurrently, my father's struggles with alcohol and marijuana worsened, casting a shadow over our household. Meanwhile, my mother's affair with our neighbor continued, adding another layer of complexity to the familial discord.

In a particularly challenging episode, my mother, working as a hotel maid, declared her need for a break. She left our home for three days, leaving my father, brother, and me to navigate the turbulent waters on our own. In the absence of her presence, essential elements of daily life, such as food, became scarce. My father, consumed by intoxication, was in no state to tend to domestic responsibilities or make necessary trips to the store. This period marked a chapter of heightened difficulty and vulnerability in our family dynamics.

During this trying period, my father's retreat to the garage became a stark symbol of his solitude, where he sought refuge in alcohol, marijuana, and the blaring tunes of classic rock. With food supplies dwindling, I took on the responsibility of preparing simple meals for my brother and me when our father was home. These makeshift meals often comprised sandwiches crafted from the limited ingredients available–typically just bread with mayonnaise or mustard.

In the initial days of my mother's absence, my brother resorted to sneaking out when our father was engrossed in his substances to find solace and sustenance at the neighbor kids' house. Meanwhile, I chose to endure hunger rather than risk asking our intoxicated father for food. The dynamic shifted, however, on the eve of my mother's return when my father surprised us with a rare treat–a pizza. It was a fleeting moment of reprieve.

After we savored the pizza, an unexpected turn unfolded. In a surprising gesture, my father, perhaps in an attempt to make a connection, invited me to join him in trying marijuana. It marked the first time he expressed interest in spending time with me. In the complexity of the situation, the allure of shared moments momentarily eclipsed my judgment. Hoping to gain the acceptance and approval of my father, I tried it.

Upon my mother's return, a disconcerting sense of déjà vu settled over the household. The familiar scent of intoxication clung to her, mirroring the aroma I associated with my father's moments of inebriation. Her entrance was marked by a silence that spoke volumes as she carried her belongings straight to the bedroom she now claimed as her own, having expelled my father.

That evening, the routine of family dinner was disrupted, with no meal prepared for my brother and me. The atmosphere grew tense, reaching a crescendo in a loud and tumultuous argument between my parents. The fallout left my father relegated to the couch for the night. Navigating the challenges of school, studies, and social interactions became an arduous task. The cloud of uncertainty surrounding what awaited me at home cast a long shadow over my daily activities, making it difficult to focus on anything other than the impending turmoil within the walls of my family home.

A few months before my 15th birthday, a rare opportunity presented itself when my mother granted permission for me to spend time with friends in town while she went shopping. Excitement filled the air as I embarked on this small venture, hoping for a respite from the usual challenges at home. However, the day took an unexpected turn when one of my friends ditched me, leaving me in the company of Susan and her brother Kevin, who I later discovered was 18. Despite the other friend's leaving, Susan and the familiarity of her presence provided a sense of safety. They extended an invitation to their house, not far from where we were. With Susan by my side, I accepted the offer, finding solace in the idea of a temporary escape from the tumultuous atmosphere that awaited me at home.

When we got there, their parents were not home, and I remember looking for them as I sat on the couch and my friend Susan left the room. Kevin offered me a glass of lemonade, so I drank some and suddenly a feeling of drowsiness came over me. The next thing I remember is waking up without clothes on in Kevin's bed, with a disorienting feeling in my head and sharp pain in my swimsuit region. When I removed the covers, there was blood on the bed and dried blood on my legs. He had drugged and raped me. The house was empty, so although I was panicked and unstable, I managed to put my clothes back on and used the phone to call my mother to pick me up.

As I shared my unsettling encounter with her, she responded with dismissive laughter and a casual accusation, saying, "You just made that up! Besides, you probably asked for it!" In the heavy silence that followed, my unspoken words hung in the air, revealing the vulnerability of a young teenager grappling with fear and confusion. My mother's reaction, void of empathy, only deepened the shadows of self-doubt cast upon me.

I had learned about sex and reproduction in eighth grade, but I was still confused and had a lot of questions. In the midst of my turbulent journey, a multitude of kind souls, seemingly sent by God, appeared to extend support in ways my parents couldn't. Despite my mother's constant dismissal, I persisted in my quest for connection with her, navigating through the repeated rejections like a persistent seeker of warmth in a cold and distant landscape.

The tongue can bring death or life;
those who love to talk will reap the consequences.
Proverbs 18:21 NLT

Do not envy evil people or desire their company.
For their hearts plot violence,

and their words always stir up trouble.
Proverbs 24: 1-2 NLT

Against the tumultuous backdrop of my freshman year in high school, the air in our home crackled with tension. Daily, my parents engaged in heated arguments, and our neighbor who committed adultery with my mother also got into violent encounters with my father. Amidst the chaos, I found myself unwittingly entangled in a poignant scene one evening. The ominous knock on our door heralded the presence of the neighbor, his breath tainted with the acrid scent of alcohol. In his outstretched hands, two candy bars served as silent tokens, a bittersweet acknowledgment of the unspoken turmoil that bound us together. There was one for me and one for my brother, a delicate offering that transcended words.

My mother happened to be in the shower at this time. My father heard the neighbor talking to me and came to the door to confront him. They shouted and cursed at one another, and my father punched him in the face. A cacophony of chaos erupted as my mother emerged from the bathroom in a state of frenzied distress, her piercing screams slicing through the tense air. In that harrowing moment, my father stood face-to-face with both her and the neighbor, a collision of emotions and accusations converging into a chilling tableau.

Just a week later, I found myself thrust into a disconcerting episode.. A group of three girls, self-proclaimed members of a mysterious "gang," perpetually murmured about clandestine meetings and initiation rites. Politely declining their invitation, I thought the matter settled. However, the eerie aftermath unfolded after my first-period class. The trio cornered me outside the classroom, casting an ominous shadow over my ordinary school day. One girl punched me in the face and knocked me down, and the other two girls kicked me in the face and ribs while I was down. It was about 5 minutes before a teacher heard what was going on and stopped it.

Seeking solace in the nurse's office, I adorned my face with bandages and accepted the healing balm for the cuts that marred my skin. Though physically wounded, I soldiered through the remainder of the day, a silent survivor of the earlier confrontation. The journey home on the school bus became a gauntlet of humiliation, with whispers and teasing from fellow students adding salt to my wounds. When I arrived home, my father noticed my distress and inquired about the ordeal. Reliving the painful encounter, I recounted the events, and his concern deepened. He questioned whether I had fought back, to which I replied in the negative. Guided by a sense of moral principle drawn from the teachings of the Bible, I explained my choice to refrain from retaliation–a commitment to turning the other cheek and refraining from answering a fool according to his folly.

> *Do not answer a fool according to his folly,*
> *Lest you also be like him.*
> **Proverbs 26:4 NKJV**

> *But I tell you, do not resist an evil person.*
> *If anyone slaps you on the right cheek,*
> *turn them to the other cheek also.*
> **Matthew 5:39 NIV**

In response, my father remained silent for a moment, his contemplative gaze piercing through the heaviness of the air. Without uttering a word in acknowledgment of my adherence to moral principles, he pivoted to a different perspective. In a determined tone, he asserted that what I needed was to fight back. Fetching a pair of boxing gloves, he embarked on a tutorial, demonstrating punch combinations with an intensity that mirrored the conflict he perceived. An internal struggle wrestled within me as I hesitated to emulate the aggressive movements he urged upon me. I couldn't shake the conviction that such actions, however well-intentioned, contradicted the moral compass I held dear.

> *"If anyone causes one of these little ones*
> *who believes in Me to stumble,*
> *it would be better for them to have a large millstone*
> *hung around their neck*
> *and to be drowned in the depths of the sea."*
> **Matthew 18:6 NIV**

As my reluctance to embrace the pugilistic lessons became apparent, my father's frustration manifested in a stern declaration. "If you do not learn to fight, you are going to be a spineless wimp your whole life!" he asserted, his words hanging heavily in the room. The ultimatum continued, with a veiled threat of punishment should a similar situation unfold again. His words cut through me, a sharp pang of hurt resonating with the realization that the lessons he sought to impart contradicted my understanding of right and wrong. In that moment, a conflict of values emerged, leaving me torn between a father's admonition and an internal compass that resisted the notion of responding to adversity with aggression.

The tongue can bring death or life;
those who love to talk will reap the consequences.
Proverbs 18:21 NLT

Navigating the labyrinth of conflicting emotions and principles, I recalled the commandment to obey my mother and father. In reluctant compliance, I engaged in practicing punches with my father, a pragmatic measure to prepare for potential future confrontations. The unspoken understanding lingered in the air, a shared secret born out of necessity.

Contemplating the consequences of my actions, I broached a delicate question with my father, seeking guidance. "What if I get in trouble for fighting back?" I inquired, my uncertainty mirrored in my gaze.

In response, he assured me, "I will make sure you get out of it," a promise that held a mix of reassurance and ambiguity. However, a condition accompanied this pact–silence. My father implored me not to divulge this to my mother, a request steeped in the desire to avoid further complications on the home front. Fearing the repercussions of disobedience, I adhered to his plea and kept the truth concealed.

A few months shy of my 16th birthday, my father summoned my brother and me to the living room one day after school. We gathered there, awaiting his arrival from work, just 30 minutes ahead of our mother's return. Settling into a serious tone, he expressed his regret that we had been unwitting witnesses to the tumultuous arguments between him and our mother. In a pivotal moment, he chose transparency, disclosing to my brother the painful truth of our mother's infidelity with the neighbor.

With a heavy heart, he revealed his profound unhappiness in the marriage and disclosed his intention to ask for a divorce when our mother returned from work. As the weight of the impending change hung in the air, my brother and I reassured him of our unwavering love, urging him to follow the path he deemed necessary for his own well-being.

The atmosphere at the dinner table during that crucial conversation was palpably awkward, a heavy silence punctuating the revelation of life-altering decisions. My father, choosing this seemingly mundane setting, mustered the courage to broach the topic, making it an unavoidable tableau for my brother and me. As the weight of impending divorce hung in the air, my mother's apparent relief surfaced when my father finally asked the question. Her confirmation that she had already procured divorce papers added a layer of finality to the revelation. In the midst of this familial upheaval, my brother expressed his desire to live with our father, revealing a glimpse of his chosen path. Feeling a pang of sympathy for my mother, I tentatively voiced my decision: "I guess I will try to live with Mom." My father, understanding the gravity of the moment, offered a lifeline–the assurance that if I ever changed my mind, a simple phone call would bridge the gap between us.

The aftermath of my parents' divorce unfolded swiftly, with my father wasting no time in extricating himself from the family home. Within two weeks, he orchestrated a move, securing an apartment and relocating with my brother. I was left behind, and life with my mother became a desolate landscape marked by her emotional absence. Her presence, when she was home, was characterized by a palpable distance. Our interactions were strained, reduced to mere formality, and she retreated to her room for solitary dinners and television, denying me entry into that isolated sanctuary. The breaking point came after a day of playing outside when I returned to find my once-secure haven transformed into chaos. My mother had ransacked my belongings, scattering them throughout my room.

Overwhelmed by the emotional toll, I reached out to my father in tears, pleading for refuge and understanding. However, my mother, in a symbolic act of closure, had changed the locks on all the doors. Undeterred, my father came to my rescue, helping me gain access to my essentials, including my birth certificate and social security card–vital tools for navigating a new chapter. In the process, I discovered my mother had locked away my baby pictures, prompting me to seize a few for the sake of cherished memories as I embarked on a journey to rebuild a sense of stability.

Transitioning to life at my father's apartment offered a marginal improvement from the strained atmosphere of my mother's home, but it wasn't devoid of its challenges. An unsettling discovery unfolded as I observed my father spending prolonged evenings at the bar, a routine that raised concerns about his well-being. The first tangible sign of change came one morning when the resonant voice of a woman emanated from my father's bedroom. A mysterious blonde woman emerged, a stranger whose intentions seemed dubious. As she prepared to leave, I couldn't suppress the unease and candidly expressed my skepticism about her motives, suggesting that she might be taking advantage of our father.

After her departure, I confided in my father, conveying my reservations. However, my concerns were met with dismissal. He attributed my apprehension to lingering anger from the divorce and dropped a bombshell—he intended to marry her after just one date. This revelation left me grappling with the rapidity of this decision.

The upheaval in my life continued with astonishing speed mere months after my 16th birthday, during the summer following my sophomore year in high school. My father, in a whirlwind decision, packed up my brother and me, leading us to merge with the life of this new woman and her three children. The abruptness of the move was underscored by the fact that they got married the very next day. However, the initial optimism surrounding the union swiftly dissipated as the reality of our new family dynamic unfolded. The woman, now my stepmother, proved to be unkind, particularly towards my brother and me. In a stark display of her disregard, my brother was relegated to sleeping on the couch, deprived of any semblance of privacy. As for me, I was assigned a futon in the garage, an arrangement that mirrored the lack of personal space. Unbeknownst to us, our stepmother was in the midst of her own recent divorce, and the ensuing drama with her ex-husband and children cast a shadow over our new living situation, compounding the challenges we faced.

The convergence of two fractured families brought with it a barrage of dysfunction that my brother and I found ourselves caught in the middle of. The complex dynamics within my new stepmother's family unveiled a tapestry of discord, a stark contrast to the stability we sought amidst our parents' divorces. The turbulence extended beyond the immediate step-sibling relationships, encompassing the residual impact of both parents' divorces. My new stepsister and stepbrothers, grappling with the aftermath of their own familial upheavals, introduced additional layers of disturbance into our lives. The transition from the dysfunction of my birth mother's household to the newfound complexities of my stepmother's family created a continuous thread of challenges, as we navigated the tumultuous waters of our own parents' divorces while being ensnared in the web of our blended family's struggles.

Vindicate me, my God,
and plead my cause against an unfaithful nation.
Rescue me from those who are deceitful and wicked.
Psalm 43:1 NIV

As a 17-year-old navigating the challenges of senior year in high school, I took a significant step towards independence by acquiring my learner's permit. Utilizing the funds earned from a summer job at the cannery after my junior year, I purchased a car from my oldest step-brother. However, the car came without an engine, prompting me to invest the money I had saved into procuring a used engine, with my father providing essential assistance in the process. Through collaborative efforts, my father and I successfully installed the engine, breathing life into the car. I dedicated myself to practicing driving, honing my skills behind the wheel of both my newly resurrected car and my father's vehicle. Feeling sufficiently prepared, I embarked on the journey to obtain my driver's license, only to face the disappointment of falling short by two points.

Undeterred, I approached my stepmother with a request to retry the driving test in two weeks. However, her response, a resounding "No way," added a layer of frustration to the setback, temporarily delaying my quest for independence on the road.

Despite the discouragement I faced in my pursuit of a driver's license, I found solace and accomplishment in my academic endeavors during my senior year of high school. Having completed my required classes, I opted for two enriching electives: serving as a teacher's aide for an algebra instructor and assuming the role of a peer tutor for students grappling with reading and language skills. As a peer tutor, I had the privilege of working with a freshman named Marcos who faced challenges in reading. This experience became a deeply rewarding journey as I shared my love for reading with someone who struggled. Witnessing Marcos's progress was particularly special, culminating in him confidently reading aloud in front of the class by the end of the school year. The impact of this accomplishment resonated with me, fueling a sense of fulfillment and contributing to my growing aspiration to become an educator.

As my senior year unfolded, I juggled various responsibilities, including a seasonal job during Christmas and New Year's as a cashier at a department store. Each paycheck contributed to my ongoing savings, further solidifying my commitment to building a better future.

Graduation day arrived, a significant milestone in my life. However, the celebratory atmosphere was tempered by concerns about my paternal grandmother Ruthie's declining health. A week before the ceremony, she suffered a stroke, rallying just in time to witness me graduate, despite her ongoing struggles. In the backdrop of these personal challenges, I faced an unhappy living situation with my stepmother, whose discouraging comments and attempts to control my father added an additional layer of stress. Yet, I refused to let these negative influences steal my joy. Graduating high school marked a significant achievement, and I embraced the pride in my accomplishment, eagerly anticipating the unknown but trusting in the future that God had for me. This marked another example of my quest for identity and independence.

> *"For I know the plans I have for you", declares the LORD,*
> *"plans to prosper you and not to harm you,*
> *plans to give you hope and a future."*
> **Jeremiah 29:11 NIV**

Having completed the seasonal job at the department store, I continued my employment at the cannery. About three weeks into the summer, however, an unexpected interruption occurred when my name echoed through the loudspeaker, beckoning me to the front office. As I approached, I found my father waiting, bearing solemn news. Ruthie had suffered a heart attack, and her condition was critical. Without hesitation, my father drove me from work to the hospital, where a somber gathering of aunts, uncles, and cousins had assembled outside her room.

The gravity of the situation unfolded as we took turns entering her room. During the agonizing wait, a nurse emerged with a sobering prognosis. Having endured three strokes and three heart attacks in the past, my grandmother's heart was now weakened to a critical point. The nurse conveyed the grim likelihood that she might not survive the night, casting a pall over the gathered family.

In the waiting room of the hospital, amidst the palpable tension, I sought solace in the words of the Psalms found within the pages of a Bible. With silent tears, I directed my thoughts and prayers towards God, pleading on behalf of my ailing grandmother.

When it was finally my turn to enter her room, the sight of her frail form was a poignant reminder of the fragility of life. Her labored breathing underscored the gravity of the moment, prompting me to approach her bedside and clasp her weakened hand. In an intimate circle with my aunt, my grandmother, and myself, we joined hands and offered individual prayers for her well-being. As I spoke my heartfelt prayer for her, a profound stillness enveloped the room. Almost immediately afterward, her shallow breaths ceased, and she departed from this earthly realm, embarking on her journey to a heavenly home with Jesus. At the age of 72, my grandmother had peacefully passed away, leaving behind cherished memories and a legacy of faith.

Good people pass away;
the godly often die before their time.
But no one seems to care or wonder why.
No one seems to understand
that God is protecting them
from the evil to come.
For those who follow godly paths
will rest in peace when they die.
Isaiah 57:1-2 NLT

Chapter Four

LOST SHEEP

All of us, like sheep, have gone astray,
each of us has turned to his own way;
But the LORD has caused
the wrongdoing of us all to fall on Him.
Isaiah 53:6 NASB

This marks a pivotal point in which I was trying desperately to find my place of belonging and where I would find my identity and purpose. At 18, still grappling with the heartache of losing my paternal grandmother, I found myself confronted with another upheaval. Just over a week after Ruthie's passing, I inadvertently overheard a conversation between my stepmother and father. To my dismay, it became apparent that my stepmother was pushing for my swift departure from the house. The evening took an unexpected turn when, after dinner, my father approached me. He conveyed that he believed it was time for me to move out and instructed me to be gone by the following morning before my stepmother left for work at 7 am. Initial feelings of anger swirled within me, but soon a realization dawned—this was an opportunity to escape the dysfunction that had characterized my living situation.

In a moment of resolve, I hastily packed a backpack with a few belongings, leaving behind the rest. The prospect of freedom from the toxic environment outweighed any sense of loss, propelling me toward an uncertain but liberating journey beyond the confines of my father and stepmother's dysfunctional home.

The sudden eviction from my father and stepmother's home left me facing a harsh reality, compounded by the fact that I didn't yet possess my driver's license. This meant leaving behind my car and relinquishing my job at the cannery, rendering me officially homeless. Determined to find refuge, I embarked on an 11-mile journey on foot to reach the gas station where my brother was employed.

After I shared my plight with him, my brother extended a temporary haven, securing permission from his roommates for me to stay a few nights. Sleeping on the floor in his living arrangement was a brief respite, lasting about a week before other circumstances necessitated my departure. The subsequent nights were spent outdoors, finding makeshift shelter on park benches, where the unsettling reality of homelessness exposed me to its perils. The vulnerability of my situation became evident as I occasionally woke to the unsettling presence of other homeless individuals attempting to pilfer my backpack. This newfound existence, thrusting me into independence at such a young age, proved to be a terrifying experience, marking the beginning of a challenging and uncertain journey.

Navigating the challenges of life on the streets exposed me to a spectrum of individuals, each with their own motives and intentions. Some proved to be kind and helpful, offering a glimmer of support in the midst of my struggles. However, there were others with selfish motives and ill intentions, preying on the vulnerabilities of someone in my situation. Lacking the foundational wisdom, guidance, and teaching that often shape one's early years, my journey was marked by the absence of sound advice and mentorship. While I had the privilege of minimal time with my paternal grandmother, many of my life lessons had to be learned the hard way. The grief from losing her, coupled with lingering emotions toward my mother, father, and stepmother, added layers of complexity to my already tumultuous experience.

The palpable insecurities and vulnerabilities I carried were apparent to those around me, making me a target for exploitation by individuals who sensed my desperation. This chapter of my life was characterized by a profound sense of loss, confusion about the direction of my life, and a harsh realization that many lessons would be learned through trial and error.

> *Be alert and of a sober mind.*
> *Your enemy the devil prowls around like a roaring lion*
> *looking for someone to devour.*
> *Resist him, standing firm in the faith,*
> *because you know that the family of believers*
> *throughout the world*
> *are undergoing the same kind of sufferings.*
> **1 Peter 5:8-9 NIV**

In the cramped confines of her makeshift dwelling, an overwhelming array of possessions competed for space, each one seemingly reluctant to yield ground. A discordant symphony of disorder echoed in every corner, while the pungent aroma of neglect lingered in the air. My visit extended only to a brief sip of water and a hasty restroom break, after which I tactfully took my leave.

On a bus journey one afternoon, my modest savings in tow, serendipity unfolded as I struck up a conversation with a fellow traveler—a woman cradling her infant son. Curiosity guided her inquiries about my purpose and destination, and with candor, I revealed my homelessness, attributing my aimless bus ride to a desire for diversion. In a spontaneous act of compassion, she extended an invitation to disembark at her stop and spend a night or two on her and her roommate's couch, provided I lend a hand in tidying up their cluttered abode. I accepted the offer, and upon reaching their apartment, I found myself navigating through a labyrinth of disorder and chaos, reminiscent of a hoarder's haven. The limited space prompted me to express my intent to use the restroom before commencing the arduous task of cleaning.

Upon the roommate's arrival, he offered a courteous introduction, and I promptly inquired about the whereabouts of the cleaning supplies. The woman retrieved them, laying them on the floor amidst the crowded chaos, as there was no available counter space amid the dirty dishes.

Deciding to tackle the kitchen first, I embarked on a marathon of dish-washing that stretched for an hour and a half, eventually conquering the entire culinary realm, including the daunting task of disposing of towering heaps of trash that ultimately filled the dumpster. The solo endeavor spanned a lengthy 2 ½ hours. Following this large effort, I permitted myself a brief respite, carving out a small sanctuary on the couch for a nap, securing my head atop my backpack. My awakening coincided with the surreal sight of the male roommate engrossed in video games, only wearing his underwear. Politely declining his offer to join him, I gathered my belongings and departed, eager to escape the peculiar scene.

Persisting in my nomadic existence, I found respite a day or two later when I encountered Harry, a man ambling with his dog. Engaging in conversation, Harry exuded politeness and respect, extending an unexpected offer: the use of his restroom for a much-needed shower and laundry session. Grateful for the chance to shed the grime accumulated during several days of sidewalk and park bench rest, I eagerly loaded my clothes into his washer and dryer, clutching the only clean ensemble for post-shower relief. Behind the locked bathroom door, my anticipation turned to shock as an unexpected visitor brushed against my ankle—the unmistakable presence of a sizable snake. A piercing scream escaped my lips as I hastily exited the shower, shrouding myself in a towel. Responding to the commotion, Harry inquired from outside the door, and upon learning about the serpentine surprise, he entered the restroom, snake-handling skills in tow. To my disbelief, it turned out to be Harry's pet snake. While a strange revelation, the incident left me wondering whether the unexpected shower guest was, in fact, a misguided attempt to catch a glimpse of my naked vulnerability.

Beware of false prophets
who come to you in sheep's clothing,
but inwardly they are ravenous wolves.
You will know them by their fruits.
Matthew 7:15-16 NKJV

Feeling uneasy after the shower ordeal, I found myself in an even more uncomfortable situation when Harry, wearing only his boxers, attempted to encroach on my personal space on the couch. With no alternative clothes available, I concocted an excuse, expressing a desire to step outside for some fresh air alone. Perched outdoors, I waited patiently until my garments emerged from the dryer.

Expressing gratitude to Harry for his hospitality, I handed over the only $5 bill in my possession, signaling my intention to leave. However, he stood in the doorway, an unspoken insistence that I linger. I firmly asserted my need to depart. Harry extended an invitation to stay for dinner, which I declined with a polite "no thank you." Striding a few blocks down the road, I glimpsed Harry's vehicle trailing behind me. He rolled down the window, suggesting I could change my mind and telling me he'd leave his door unlocked. I distanced myself as much as possible, but I'd encounter Harry again in the near future.

Embarking on a bus journey downtown, I serendipitously encountered Rachel, a school friend. I shared about the unsettling encounter with Harry, and she empathetically extended an invitation to accompany her to her parents' house, where she was still residing. I gratefully accepted her offer, and we spent the day together, finding solace in each other's company.

As evening descended, Rachel expressed a desire to venture out, and I proposed a visit to the local pool hall to shoot some pool alongside our mutual friend Jared. Together, we embraced the opportunity for a light-hearted and enjoyable evening, putting the harrowing experiences of the recent past behind us.

At the pool hall, the atmosphere buzzed with the presence of familiar faces from school. Outside, as we gathered for a few moments, Rachel produced a marijuana joint from her pocket, suggesting we indulge before engaging in a game of pool. I succumbed to peer pressure, having tried it only once before with my father. Rachel, Jared, and I took a few puffs. The disorienting effects left me feeling slightly dizzy.

As we prepared to leave, I spotted Harry. Despite recognizing me, he feigned ignorance of our previous encounter. Harry engaged in conversation with Jared and other friends, persuading them to join a "party" at his place. Unsettled by the proposition, I felt a strong sense of discomfort, but my commitment to spending the night with Rachel compelled me to navigate through the unfolding situation.

When we got to his apartment, some of Harry's friends were already there, and some of them were taking turns snorting white powder up their noses with a straw. I had never before been exposed to this, but I could tell they were doing drugs of some sort.

I chose a spot on the couch beside Rachel. She produced a marijuana pipe from her purse, and Harry, ever eager, offered to load it with some marijuana. As the pipe circulated among us, I took a single puff, only to notice an unusual taste and sensation. A sudden wave of discomfort swept over me, and shortly thereafter, Rachel expressed a similar unease. Concerned, we sought refuge in food and water, finding a modicum of relief, but the unsettling suspicion lingered that Harry had laced the marijuana with another substance.

Deciding it was best to leave, we concocted an excuse about wanting to step outside for a cigarette. Both recognizing the potential danger, Rachel and I began to walk away, only to have Harry spot us and give chase. The adrenaline-fueled escape was a harrowing experience, leaving both Rachel and me shaken by the realization that we had narrowly evaded a potentially perilous situation orchestrated by Harry.

In the aftermath of the unsettling encounters, I chose to venture out on my own. Seeking solace and reflection, I took a moment to connect with God. In prayer, I earnestly sought His forgiveness, acknowledging the poor choices that had led me into challenging and potentially dangerous situations. It was a humble plea for guidance and strength to navigate the uncertainties ahead.

If we confess our sins,
He is faithful and just to forgive our sins,
and to cleanse us from all unrighteousness.
1 John 1:9 KJV

I decided I was done with the distractions, so I started applying for jobs, even though I found myself homeless. After enduring another month of sleeping outside, I unexpectedly encountered Tracy, an old friend from my first high school. Tracy, a clean and sober companion, was commuting on the bus. She shared that she had her own apartment and generously offered me a temporary stay until I received responses from the job applications I had submitted.

Gratefully accepting Tracy's kind offer, I found myself sleeping on her couch. Using Tracy's landline phone number as my contact, I applied for a position at a local burger restaurant. To my surprise, they called me for an interview the very next day. I went in and, to my joy, secured the job just before my 19th birthday.

With Tracy's supportive assistance, I extended my stay for a few more days. Encouraged by the newfound stability, I gathered the courage to approach Tracy's apartment manager and inquire about the possibility of qualifying for an apartment. I shared my recent employment success and explained my challenging circumstances.

The apartment manager elaborated that the building was HUD-subsidized, with eligibility determined by income. Realizing I met the criteria, I eagerly applied. To my delight, I soon discovered that I had been approved for the apartment. Remarkably, I secured a residence just across the complex from Tracy.

Despite my past missteps, I sought redemption, taking responsibility for my actions. With determination and effort, I embraced a new beginning. Graced by a positive turn of events, I found stability in both my living situation and newfound employment.

Let us then approach God's throne
of grace with confidence,
so that we may receive mercy
and find grace to help us in our time of need.
Hebrews 4:16 NIV

And my God will liberally supply (fill until full)
your every need
according to His riches
in glory in Christ Jesus.
Philippians 4:19 AMP

In the span of ten months, I transitioned from homelessness to having both a home and steady employment, all by the grace of God. I acquired a landline telephone and even seized the opportunity to get my first cell phone through a discount promotion from the phone company. Slowly but surely, with the kindness of others, I began to furnish my new space.

Acts of generosity surrounded me: an elderly neighbor offered me her couch, a colleague at the restaurant contributed a futon and nightstand, and my studio apartment happened to be conveniently close to the hotel where my mother still worked. One day, as I disembarked from the bus after work, my mother spotted me and beckoned me over. Despite lingering hurt from our past, I mustered the courage to share my recent accomplishments with her—a job and an apartment. To my surprise, she offered to buy me a McDonald's chicken sandwich and a drink, a simple yet meaningful gesture. Then, she presented me with a belated birthday present, acknowledging the birthdays she had missed over the past few years. In the trunk of her car, she revealed a small wooden hope chest, expressing her hope that I had room for it in my apartment. In that moment, a sense of compassion for my mother welled up within me. I hugged her, expressed my gratitude, and shared my contact information. For a moment, as we stood there with the hope chest between us, it seemed like a turning point—a glimmer of optimism that perhaps we could mend things between us.

> *Love bears all things,*
> *believes all things,*
> *hopes all things,*
> *endures all things.*
> *Love never ends.*
> **1 Corinthians 13:7-8 ESV**

Chapter Five

BROKEN

With a full-time job, a stable apartment, and support from Tracy, I began to feel a growing sense of confidence. Encouraged by what seemed like an improved relationship with my mother, I decided to take a significant step forward and applied for financial aid to enroll in classes at a local community college, where Tracy was already pursuing a language arts course. However, my optimism took a hit when the woman in the financial aid office informed me that, being under the age of 25, I needed my parents to co-sign the forms. This news caused my heart to sink, knowing it would necessitate reaching out to both my father and my mother—a prospect that filled me with a mix of apprehension and uncertainty.

In the midst of the daunting task of securing support for my college education, I reluctantly dialed my father's number, bracing for the call I had been dreading the most. Surprisingly, he willingly provided the necessary information for the form, showing an unexpected willingness to support my pursuit of higher education. However, when I mustered the courage to share my intentions with my mother and asked for her assistance in completing her part of the financial aid forms, the atmosphere shifted drastically. She became defensive and adamantly refused to contribute. In a hurtful tirade, she questioned the need for my college ambitions, dismissing them by saying that I was stupid and would not make anything important of my life, and even telling me that the rape at 14 was my fault. The painful reminder of her skepticism and disapproval shattered my hope for a meaningful connection with her. Despite her subsequent attempts to reach out, I chose to maintain a distance, recognizing that, despite her efforts, God had shown that her heart remained unchanged.

Dear friends, do not believe everyone
who claims to speak by the Spirit.
You must test them
to see if the spirit they have comes from God.
For there are many false prophets in the world.
1 John 4:1 NLT

In the aftermath of that emotional blow from my mother, my self-esteem plummeted even further. While I was in that vulnerable state, Tracy and I encountered a man named Nathan during a girls' day out. Despite Nathan appearing older, he exuded a down-to-earth demeanor. He introduced us to his friends and eventually suggested we visit his place. We agreed, and once there, he started mixing alcoholic cocktails for everyone. Tracy, unfamiliar with alcohol, succumbed to the temptation and had two cocktails. She was soon unconscious on the floor. As I tried to rouse Tracy to leave, Nathan expressed his fondness for me and urged me to stay. Blinded by my own emotional turmoil, I did. This marked the inception of a series of toxic relationships for me.

Like a dog that returns to his vomit
is a fool who repeats his foolishness.
Proverbs 26:11 NLT

Entranced by Nathan's charm and his adept ability to say "all the right things," I found myself entangled in a relationship with him for a few months. During this period, I crossed paths with Pauline, a friend visiting her boyfriend's family from another state. We quickly developed a strong friendship. As Nathan continued to woo me, showcasing his guitar-playing skills and expressing grand plans, he mentioned a weekend road trip to Alabama. Somehow, swayed by his persuasive words, I agreed to accompany him. Upon reaching Alabama, fatigue took hold of me on the first night when we went to check into the hotel. Exhausted, I inadvertently left my bags in his car, setting the stage for an unexpected turn of events.

Amidst my weariness that night, Nathan attempted to persuade me into a sexual encounter, but I firmly communicated that I wasn't ready to take that step in our relationship. Seeming to understand, he agreed to retire for the night. However, the next morning, as I searched for my clothes, I made a shocking discovery. The passenger side car window, where I had left my belongings, was shattered, and all my possessions were gone. Attempting to report the theft to the Alabama police proved futile, as they dismissed it, citing it as a common occurrence they no longer bothered to address.

Upon returning home the very next day, I woke up to a note on my apartment door from Nathan. It revealed that he had met another woman during our trip and was ending our relationship. Shockingly, I later learned that he had been involved with this other woman throughout our time together and they swiftly got married. The painful truth of his deception added another layer to the heartbreak and betrayal I experienced during that tumultuous period of my life.

Following the tumultuous chapter with Nathan, another figure swiftly entered my life, introduced by Tracy–a man named Richard. As I spent time with him and a few other friends, Richard mentioned that they were passing through from another state. As Tracy and I bid farewell to him, Tracy hinted that Richard had something to ask me. In that moment, Richard expressed his admiration, claiming that he found me to be the most beautiful girl he had ever met. I was vulnerable, grappling with my self-esteem; his compliment, even if momentarily deceptive, led me to say yes to his invitation for a date.

Such people are not serving Christ our Lord;
they are serving their own personal interests.
By smooth talk and glowing words,
they deceive innocent people.
Romans 16:18 NLT

Richard went above and beyond to impress me. Showering me with
expensive jewelry, stylish clothing, and fancy meals, he created an illusion
of opulence. Amidst this whirlwind of attention, I found myself gaining
about 20 pounds. Around this time, Pauline visited my apartment when
Richard was present. She shared the joyful news of her impending
marriage to her boyfriend Gerald in Hawaii and invited me to stay at her
mother's house for the wedding, even asking me to be a bridesmaid.
Richard, always eager to please, purchased a bridesmaid's dress for me and
arranged for our airline tickets to Hawaii.

The wedding turned out to be a delightful experience. However, the
joy was tempered when, on the day before we were scheduled to fly back, I
received a call on my cell phone from a neighbor at my apartment
complex. The news was alarming–our units had caught fire. Hastening
home, I discovered a small hole in the front door, hastily patched with
plywood, and minor smoke damage inside. Miraculously, everything was
fine, and the apartment remained intact. Grateful and relieved, I
attributed the safety of my home to God, offering praise and glory
to Him.

Enter His gates with thanksgiving
and His courts with praise,
give thanks to Him and
praise His Name.
Psalm 100:4 NIV

Despite Richard's smooth talk and lavish gestures, an underlying
misery persisted within me. Unable to summon the courage to express my
true feelings, I kept my emotional struggles concealed. After two months
of dating, Richard expressed a desire for me to meet his parents. I visited
his home state and met his mother and stepfather. While they were polite,

they seemed to lack genuine interest in Richard's life. During a moment alone with his mother, she conveyed a mixed message. She expressed that she liked me and found me beautiful but suggested that I should lose some weight. This comment, coupled with the internal turmoil I was experiencing, added to the complexity of my emotions during this period of my life.

The comment from Richard's mother hit me deeply, though I concealed my hurt feelings. When Richard brought me home, I shared the encounter with him and expressed how her words affected me. To my astonishment, he disclosed that he had realized he was gay and attracted to men, bringing our relationship to an abrupt end. The combination of this rejection and the weight-related criticism from his mother plunged me into severe depression. During this dark period, I withdrew from life, going only between work and home. Struggling with my emotions, I stopped eating for weeks, resorting to an unhealthy reliance on diet pills in excess of the recommended dosage. The rapid weight loss, coupled with the detrimental effects of the pills and malnutrition, took a toll on my health. Attempts to reintroduce food into my diet were met with diffi-culty, as I couldn't keep anything down for several days, exacerbating my physical and emotional distress.

Despite successfully shedding the 20 pounds I had gained, and a few extra, my depression persisted. I spent days lethargically lying around my apartment, punctuated by moments of smoking marijuana when not at work. One day, a knock echoed through my apartment, and upon opening the door, I was surprised to find Jared accompanied by a tall, silent young man with tattoos named Irvin. Jared explained that he remembered my interest in getting tattoos and thought to introduce me to Irvin, who was a tattoo artist.

I couldn't help but express my discomfort, questioning why Jared had brought Irvin to my home without prior permission. Jared meant well–he explained that he wanted to facilitate a connection based on my past mention of an interest in tattoos. However, this unexpected visit added a layer of complexity to an already tumultuous period in my life. I asked them to leave.

The next day, Jared called to suggest I visit on my day off. Jared picked me up and took me to his parents' house, where Irvin was present. My initial impression of Irvin had been unfavorable, and I chose to ignore him due to the discomfort he had caused.

Eventually, Irvin approached me, inquiring about my connection with Jared. I was candid about my feelings, expressing my discomfort and dislike towards Irvin. Initially hurt by my honesty, Irvin began opening up about the challenges he faced, including shyness, struggles with bipolar disorder, and witnessing his mother endure physical and emotional abuse from his father, who appeared psychotic. As Irvin shared more about his life, I found a newfound empathy and decided to discuss the possibility of getting a tattoo from him.

Talking to Irvin about his struggles created a connection that, at the time, seemed promising, but eventually unfolded into a dark and malevolent influence. Despite my ongoing depression stemming from past traumas and the pain inflicted by other men, I had not yet invited the Lord into my heart. This vulnerability created an opening for the enemy to exploit through Irvin, who, laden with his own baggage, became a destructive force in my life. The absence of a spiritual anchor in my grandmother, compounded by the weight of past hurts, allowed the enemy to take hold and cast a shadow over my journey.

"I am the Door;
anyone who enters through Me will be saved
(and will live forever),
and will go in and out (freely),
and find pasture (spiritual security).
The thief comes only in order
to steal and kill and destroy;
I came that they may have and enjoy life,
and have it in abundance (to the full, till it overflows)."
John 10:9-10 AMP

Despite the warning signs and the information Irvin shared about his struggles with bipolar disorder and his family's history of abuse, I failed to heed the red flags. When I expressed my desire for angel wings on my shoulder blades in memory of my grandmother, Irvin, lacking a studio, suggested doing the tattoo at my apartment. He offered to forgo charging me for the tattoo but requested permission to bring his best friend Trevor along.

God had been trying to guide and warn me through the details Irvin shared, but without a strong connection to the Lord, I was unable to discern the wisdom needed to make better choices. Ignoring the subtle warnings, I allowed the situation to unfold, unknowingly paving the way for unforeseen consequences.

During the initial stages of Irvin's tattoo session, Trevor requested some food. Despite my limited grocery stock, I offered what I had–Top Ramen, cereal, and a small amount of milk. Trevor consumed everything without offering replacements, prompting me to ask Irvin and Trevor to clean up the resulting mess of trash. After some hesitation, they did tidy up, but then lingered at my apartment.

As my work shift approached, I insisted that both Irvin and Trevor leave. They claimed they needed to use my phone for a ride and departed to meet their transport at the nearby grocery store. However, this marked the beginning of incessant phone calls from Irvin, requesting to "hang out" at my apartment. Despite asserting boundaries, I allowed him occasional visits on my days off, clarifying my disinterest in a romantic relationship but offering a chance at friendship. This pattern continued for about a month until Irvin confessed his feelings, asking me to be his girlfriend. Despite lacking reciprocal feelings, I conceded in a moment of weakness. Subsequently, Irvin became increasingly clingy, insisting on frequent visits even during my working hours.

On one occasion, I granted Irvin permission to stay at my place while I went to work, emphasizing the importance of not answering the door or phone and refraining from inviting anyone over. Despite his assurances that he'd comply, when I returned home around 7 pm, I discovered that Irvin had blatantly disregarded my instructions and had invited Trevor over. Upon entering the bathroom for a shower, I encountered a disarray of dirty clothes and my hand-held mirror on the floor, with what looked like crystal meth and straws in plain sight.

Feeling an overwhelming sense of disrespect and anger, I reached my breaking point upon realizing illegal drugs were being used in my home. I sternly demanded that both Irvin and Trevor leave immediately, warning of police involvement if such behavior persisted. Resolute in standing up for myself, I resisted the urge to reconsider my decision.

A week later, Irvin reached out, expressing sincere remorse for not following my instructions and pledging never to repeat the offense. He then asked for another chance. Although I had not yet committed to following Christ, the teachings of the Scriptures influenced my decision-making process.

> *Then Peter came to Him and asked,*
> *"Lord, how often should I forgive*
> *someone who sins against me? Seven times?"*
> *"No, not seven times," Jesus replied,*
> *"but seventy times seven!"*
> **Matthew 18:21-22 NLT**

Despite the challenges we faced, I chose to forgive Irvin and continue our relationship, although I maintained my decision not to allow him back into my apartment. We spent time together at his mother Greta and stepfather Alan's house, where he still resided. I was 21 years old, and I decided to inquire about Irvin's age. He claimed to be 20, but I later found this to be untrue. We had been together for about three months, and Irvin broached the idea of us getting an apartment together. Uncertain but open to the possibility, I agreed, considering I had been living in my current apartment for over two years. We found a newly constructed complex and applied for it, taking the next step in our relationship.

Securing the apartment was possible only because of my employment, as Irvin was not currently working. My recent job switch to a department store, where I earned more than at the previous hamburger restaurant, played a crucial role in qualifying for the new place. With this, I became solely responsible for our living situation.

I gave notice at the previous complex, initiating the process of moving into the new two-bedroom apartment. The new place, complete with a washer and dryer, felt like a significant upgrade. Despite the initial sense of hope in my relationship with Irvin, this marked the beginning of a dark and self-destructive path for me.

The first night in the new apartment went smoothly, but the

following day, I had to work a double shift from open to close to afford our living space. When I returned home at 11 pm, I was met with a chaotic scene–the apartment was in disarray, loud music echoed through the space, and Irvin had gathered at least seven friends there. Fuming with anger, I demanded an explanation. Upon entering the kitchen, my frustration peaked as I discovered a long mirror covered in crushed meth and rolled-up dollar bills used for snorting. In an attempt to address the situation, Irvin took me into his bedroom to talk.

He did not even give me a chance to say anything before he pulled a shotgun out of the closet. I was terrified when he showed me the bullets inside that were loaded. He told me in a very deep and scary voice, "You will do what I tell you to ***** or I will ****ing kill you!" He put his hand over my mouth to prevent me from screaming. I bit his hand and wriggled away to go out the door and he shoved the shotgun in my back forcefully. Then he dragged me by my hair to the bathroom sink where there was a mirror with more meth on it crushed and in a line. He handed me a rolled-up dollar bill and told me that I had better snort the meth, or he would kill me. I looked for a means of escape, but there was none. I had a loaded shotgun at my back, held by my meth addict lunatic boyfriend. I did not want to die at 21, so I did as he demanded, and I instantly felt very sick. I was in the bathroom for about 40 minutes, crying and puking in the toilet. He kicked me in the head before leaving the room.

In the aftermath of the disturbing discovery, as Irvin left the room, I found myself overwhelmed with a mix of emotions. In the midst of intense physical and emotional distress, I crawled out of the room, only to be confronted by the disarray left in the apartment. The remnants of the chaotic scene served as a stark reminder of the trust I had placed in Irvin, despite multiple warnings from God urging me to steer clear of him. Terrified and consumed by shame, I grappled with the consequences of my choices and the stark realization that I had ignored God's guidance to stay away from Irvin.

If you rebel against the LORD's commandments,
the hand of the LORD will be against you.
1 Samuel 12:15 NIV

Life took a turn for the worse from this point onward. Knowing that I had willingly indulged in methamphetamine with Irvin, I felt powerless to leave him, fearing I wouldn't have a strong defense if I attempted to break free from the toxic relationship. Despite the daunting circumstances, I resolved to devise a plan for my escape. I formulated a plan to save money from my next paycheck, intending to rent a hotel room as a temporary refuge. On the day I received my paycheck, as I made my way to the bank to deposit it, I encountered an unexpected presence outside–Irvin. I was bewildered by his sudden appearance, certain I hadn't disclosed my plans or even mentioned it was payday. Irvin claimed he wanted to spend time with me after work, trailing behind me as I proceeded.

Feeling unsettled by his unannounced presence, I voiced my discomfort, but Irvin remained silent, persisting in following me. Sensing impending danger, I opted to take a detour to a nearby 7-Eleven for a Slurpee and cigarettes before heading back to the apartment. Irvin trailed me every step of the way, exacerbating my sense of foreboding, signaling that something ominous was about to unfold.

When we got inside the apartment, he grabbed me by the hair, picked me up, and threw me against the wall. "If you ever try to leave me again, I will ****ing kill you! Remember, ***** I own you!" About an hour after the unsettling encounter with Irvin outside the bank, a knock on the door startled us. Irvin, who had just snorted a line of crystal meth, answered the door to find a police officer standing there. The officer explained that a report had been made regarding a potential abuse situation. Though I couldn't hear their conversation, somehow Irvin managed to convince the officer that everything was fine, and the officer left without further action.

The following morning, Irvin enlisted William, one of his associates in drug use, to drive me to work. Claiming he couldn't trust me anymore, Irvin accompanied us. During the first hour of my shift, I noticed Irvin lurking around the fitting room, where I worked. Another employee, Shelly, who came to relieve me for my break, inquired if Irvin was my boyfriend, sensing something was amiss.

Feeling trapped in a situation I couldn't escape, I reluctantly confirmed to Shelly that Irvin was indeed my boyfriend, but told her I couldn't divulge any further details. Upon returning home from work that evening,

I was greeted by the blaring music emanating from our apartment once again. Irvin was hosting another party, this time with even more people–nearly 15 in total. The atmosphere was chaotic, with smoking indoors (against the rules), litter strewn everywhere, and the unmistakable presence of drugs and alcohol. Overwhelmed with frustration, I retreated to my room, muffling my screams of exasperation into my pillow. I stayed hidden there for as long as possible, hoping to avoid Irvin's notice of my return.

He quickly noticed I was home (likely a friend told him), and he burst into my bedroom heavily intoxicated with both alcohol and meth. He forcibly took my clothes off and proceeded to rape me from behind with angry force, despite my cries. I woke up sore and bleeding. Feeling a sense of dread wash over me, I proceeded with my morning routine, preparing for work despite the chaos at home. As I made my way to leave on foot, I was confronted with a harsh reality: a 48-hour eviction notice plastered on our front door.

Shocked and confused, I hurried to the apartment complex's front office to seek clarification from the manager. She explained that numerous complaints about noise and disturbances during my work hours had prompted the eviction notice. Despite my recent rent payment, she insisted on collecting it again before our departure. Stunned by this demand, I protested, explaining my inability to afford another rent payment so soon after the last one. However, she remained adamant, warning that she'd take legal action if we failed to comply. Struggling to comprehend the gravity of the situation, I left the office burdened with the weight of uncertainty and impending eviction.

Amidst the turmoil and heartache, I found myself grappling with the consequences of once again ignoring God's subtle nudges to leave. Tears streamed down my face as I made my way to work, burdened by the weight of our eviction. In a desperate attempt to salvage what remained of our belongings, I sent Irvin a photo of the eviction notice, signaling the need to start packing.

Thankfully, Irvin's mother, Greta, came to our aid, assisting with the daunting task of packing up our possessions. With nowhere to call home, I made the difficult decision to secure a storage unit for our belongings, bearing the financial burden once again. Homeless and vulnerable, I utilized what little resources I had left to secure a temporary refuge–a cheap motel room for three nights.

Approaching the motel manager with our dire circumstances, I explained our situation, hoping for a glimmer of understanding. To my surprise and relief, the manager extended an offer of grace, granting us an additional night's stay until my next payday. In that moment, I couldn't help but see it as a manifestation of God's unwavering grace, a blessing I felt utterly undeserving of. Truly, I found solace in His mercy and provision during our darkest hour. Thank You, Lord.

> *Each time He said,*
> *"My grace is all you need.*
> *My power works best in weakness."*
> *So now I am glad to boast about my weaknesses,*
> *so that the power of Christ can work through me.*
> **2 Corinthians 12:9 NLT**

Chapter Six

WIDE IS THE GATE THAT LEADS TO DESTRUCTION

"Enter through the narrow gate.
For wide is the gate and broad
and easy to travel is the path
that leads to destruction and eternal loss,
and there are many who enter through it.
But small is the gate and
narrow and difficult to travel
is the path that leads the way to (everlasting) life,
and there are few who find it."
Matthew 7:13-14 AMP

During our stay in the motel, I found myself faced with the daunting task of attending the eviction court date, requiring me to take time off work. Gathering what little money I could scrape together, I mustered $475–a hundred dollars less than the rent–which I presented as an offer to the court, explaining it was the amount the landlord had requested.

To my surprise, the landlord failed to appear at the eviction court, leaving the court to address the matter without their presence. In a fortunate turn of events, the court accepted the $475 I brought as payment. It went toward the charges incurred from the damages Irvin had left behind, which totaled $800. The remaining balance of the bill was rightfully attributed to Irvin, given that he was responsible for the damage. Despite the challenging circumstances, I found a small sense of relief knowing that some form of resolution had been achieved.

As our motel stay drew to a close, Irvin's mother, Greta, informed us that she had cosigned on a duplex for us to move into. Despite knowing that Irvin was unemployed and that I would bear the burden of all expenses, she extended this gesture. With little choice, we relocated to the duplex, a modest two-bedroom dwelling in a neighborhood plagued by drug activity.

Feeling deeply unsettled and unsafe in our new surroundings, I found solace in silent prayers to God, fervently pleading for a way out of this situation and away from Irvin. Despite the grim circumstances, I held onto hope, trusting in God's provision and guidance to lead me out of the darkness enveloping my life.

No temptation has overtaken you
except what is common to mankind.
And God is faithful;
He will not let you be tempted
beyond what you can bear.
But when you are tempted,
He will also provide a way out
so that you can endure it.
1 Corinthians 10:13 NIV

Life with Irvin continued to worsen. Every day or night I came home from work, Irvin had a lot of drug addict "friends" over doing drugs, selling drugs, and giving illegal tattoos. Many of the women looked like drug-addicted prostitutes. The revelation of Irvin's true age added another layer of deception to an already tumultuous situation. Greta's unexpected arrival with a cake bearing the words "Happy 18th Birthday" for Irvin shattered any illusion I had about Irvin's honesty. The atmosphere in our duplex grew increasingly toxic as the abuse escalated. To find respite from the chaos, I often sought refuge on the couch, sacrificing my comfort to avoid the turmoil unfolding in our shared living space. Despite my efforts to carve out moments of tranquility, peace remained elusive. One particular day, on my rare day off, I retreated to the sanctuary of my bedroom, relishing the quietude and solace it provided. Separated from Irvin by the closed door, I immersed myself in the simple pleasure of reading, cherishing the fleeting moments of calm amid the storm raging around me.

Then, Irvin busted in the door, kissed me forcefully, tied my hands behind my back with zip ties, and punched and kicked me in the face and ribs. He told me that we were no longer together, and that no one would ever want to be with me when he got done with me. Then he put duct tape over my mouth, picked me up and threw me into the closet, and locked the door. The harrowing ordeal of being bound and gagged left me trembling with fear and desperation. With trembling hands, I managed to peel the duct tape off my mouth, granting me a sliver of freedom. Retrieving my cell phone from my pocket, I checked the date and time, relieved to find it was still my day off. However, the looming dread of the impending workday weighed heavily on my mind.

Tears streamed down my face silently as I grappled with the terror of Irvin discovering my escape attempt and inflicting further harm. The metallic taste of blood lingered on my lip, a painful reminder of the brutality I had endured. Hunger gnawed at my stomach, exacerbated by my emaciated state–a result of methamphetamine use, depression, and the scarcity of food in our household.

Exhausted and drained, I eventually succumbed to sleep, only to awaken abruptly, mere hours before my scheduled shift at work. With the remaining battery life on my cell phone, I mustered the courage to call my workplace, informing them of a potential delay without disclosing the horrors I had experienced. Locked in a cycle of abuse and despair, I clung to the fragile thread of hope, praying for deliverance from the nightmare consuming my life.

Finally, Trevor brought a fleeting moment of relief as he freed me from the confines of the closet. With precious little time to spare, I showered, changed my clothes, and embarked on the journey to work, albeit 15 minutes behind schedule.

My deteriorating physical condition, marked by bruises and cuts on my face, did not escape the notice of my coworkers. Concerned for my well-being, Shelly approached me during my break, expressing worry over my alarming weight loss and the visible signs of abuse. In a moment of vulnerability, I confided in her, revealing the horrors I had endured at the hands of Irvin. With compassion and empathy, she offered me refuge in her home, alongside her husband, Victor, and their young child.

Grateful for the lifeline extended to me, I acknowledged the need for a carefully crafted escape plan. Necessities from our shared residence and the urgency of my situation necessitated meticulous planning. Recognizing the importance of safety, I agreed to Shelly's condition of obtaining a restraining order against Irvin to ensure my protection in their home. As I braced myself for the impending upheaval, I resolved to seize this opportunity as a fresh start, guided by the support and kindness of newfound allies.

In the midst of chaos and uncertainty, I couldn't help but feel God was guiding my steps toward freedom. As I returned home that evening, the sight of Irvin and the other women passed out from a prolonged drug binge reinforced my resolve to break free from his toxic grip.

In a stroke of serendipity, one of Irvin's friends, Cory, provided the perfect distraction. While Irvin and Cory engaged in their drug-related dealings, I seized the opportunity to slip away unnoticed, my heart pounding with a mixture of fear and anticipation. With my backpack clenched tightly to my chest, I tiptoed out the front door, leaving behind the suffocating confines of a life overshadowed by abuse and addiction.

As I stepped into the cool night air, a sense of liberation washed over me, buoyed by the belief that God had orchestrated this moment of escape. With each step away from that dark chapter of my life, I embraced the promise of a brighter future, guided by faith and fueled by the courage to reclaim my autonomy and rebuild my life anew.

Amidst the bustling streets teeming with fellow lost souls, fear and uncertainty gripped me as I navigated the unfamiliar terrain alone. Yet, a glimmer of inner strength propelled me forward, each step a testament to my determination to break free from the shackles of my past.

Seeking refuge and guidance, I found solace in the welcoming glow of a Plaid Pantry store, where I used the payphone to reach out to Shelly.

With her reassuring voice guiding me, I embarked on a journey across town, summoning a cab with the meager funds I had on hand. Arriving at Shelly's haven, I collapsed onto her couch, exhausted and drained, but finally safe. As I emerged from the haze of drugs and starvation, Shelly's nurturing care provided a beacon of hope in my darkest hour. Nourished by her kindness and nourishing food, I began to reclaim my strength and sense of self. Embracing my newfound role as a caretaker for their son Nigel while Shelly and Victor tended to their responsibilities, I found purpose and stability in the midst of chaos.

However, as my hours at the department store dwindled, the need to contribute financially weighed heavily on my shoulders. Determined to secure steady employment, I ventured out into the world, where chance encounters led me to Kassidy, Steve, and Chuck—kindred spirits offering companionship and camaraderie in the face of adversity.

In celebration of Chuck's milestone birthday, I joined him and Steve at a strip club, ensuring Chuck's enjoyment while abstaining from alcohol myself. As I watched Chuck revel in the festivities, I couldn't help but reflect on the winding path that had led me here, grateful for the newfound connections and glimmers of joy amidst the darkness of my past.

Amidst the fervor of the strip club atmosphere, the pulsating music and raucous cheers of the crowd filled the air as dollar bills rained down onto the stage. Caught up in the excitement, I found myself at the center of attention when Lula, a dancer with ample assets, pulled me onto the stage. Faced with the unexpected request to bare myself to the audience, I hesitated, feeling the weight of their collective anticipation bearing down on me. Despite my initial reluctance, the relentless chants urging me to succumb to their demands echoed in my ears, drowning out my inner reservations. Yielding to the pressure, I offered a fleeting glimpse of my bare chest to the eager crowd before being swiftly escorted offstage by Lula. As I caught my breath, I found myself face to face with Rick, the club owner, who extended an enticing offer for me to join the ranks of the dancers. Though apprehensive about the proposition, the promise of potential earnings beckoned in the midst of my financial uncertainty. Encouraged by Lula's reassurance and the prospect of securing another source of income, I resolved to seize the opportunity, despite the uneasy feeling gnawing at the pit of my stomach.

Entering into the unfamiliar world of exotic dancing, I hastily assembled a wardrobe of short skirts, crop tops, and high heels, unsure of the standard attire for such establishments. On my first day, faced with the requirement to adopt a stage name, I found myself at a loss. Without hesitation, the manager dubbed me Barbie, drawing attention to my blond pixie cut styled with spikes and likening me to a punk rock rendition of the iconic doll.

Thus began a journey into a new persona, one crafted within the confines of the strip club. It offered a semblance of identity detached from reality. While the moniker bestowed upon me conveyed a sense of uniqueness, it also served as a guise, masking the inherent degradation of the profession. In the midst of societal judgment and personal turmoil, it became a shield of sorts, a facade intended to provide security and distance from past traumas, particularly the specter of Irvin looming in the shadows. Yet, beneath the veneer of glamor and allure, I grappled with the dissonance of my newfound identity, recognizing the inherent contradictions and compromises it entailed.

The day following my debut as a dancer, Shelly accompanied me to the courthouse at dawn to initiate the process of obtaining a restraining order against Irvin. Though a mixture of fear and determination coursed through me, Shelly's unwavering support served as a beacon of strength, reassuring me that I was taking the necessary steps to safeguard myself. I found courage in her words, her presence a steadfast reminder that I was not alone in this daunting journey. As we embarked on this crucial endeavor, Shelly's encouragement echoed in my ears, instilling in me the belief that I was indeed making the right decision, and that safety and security awaited on the other side of this harrowing ordeal.

"It is the LORD who goes before you.
He will be with you;
he will not leave you or forsake you.
Do not fear or be dismayed."
Deuteronomy 31:8 ESV

With trembling resolve, I bared my soul to the officials at the court-house, recounting every harrowing detail of my history of abuse at the hands of Irvin. In a swift and merciful gesture, the court granted me a restraining order, a legal shield protecting me from Irvin's malevolent presence for the next three years. Armed with this newfound sense of protection, I was assured that if Irvin dared to breach the mandated 50-foot boundary, swift justice would be served, and law enforcement would intervene, ensuring his apprehension and removal from my vicinity.

Guided by Shelly's comforting presence, I ventured to Irvin's residence, accompanied by a police officer tasked with aiding in the retrieval of my belongings. Despite the gravity of the situation, I faced Irvin and his cohorts with a mixture of trepidation and defiance. As Shelly and the officer ventured inside to assist me, I braved the disdainful stares and mocking laughter emanating from Irvin and his drugged-out companions. In that moment, I stood firm, reclaiming a semblance of power and agency in the face of adversity, determined to break free from the shackles of fear and reclaim what was rightfully mine.

Amidst the remnants of my former life strewn haphazardly in Irvin's residence, I found solace in the small treasures salvaged from the wreckage —a few articles of clothing, drawing pads and pencils, and my makeup. Yet, the absence of my prized possessions—my laptop, CDs, DVDs, and other personal effects—served as a stark reminder of the irrevocable losses incurred, likely traded or stolen in the grip of addiction. While the physical distance from Irvin and the toxic environment of drugs and abuse brought a sense of relief, an overwhelming emptiness gnawed at my core. Despite the newfound freedom, the scars of trauma ran deep, leaving behind a void that seemed insurmountable.

However, the semblance of peace was short-lived. Irvin's mother, Greta, unleashed a barrage of harassing calls and threatening texts, demanding payment for rent and bills left unpaid. Faced with this new wave of intimidation, I refused to succumb to fear, instead taking decisive action by alerting the authorities to Greta's relentless harassment. The intervention of law enforcement served as a temporary reprieve, quelling the onslaught of threats and enabling me to reclaim a semblance of control over my life amidst the chaos.

Amidst the neon glow of the strip club, I found a semblance of financial stability, pocketing a substantial sum each night—an average of $200 to $300, sometimes even more. Buoyed by this newfound income, Shelly, Victor, and I seized the opportunity to upgrade our living situation, relocating to a larger apartment situated conveniently close to public transportation and, more importantly, farther away from Irvin's influence.

Though my spiritual journey had yet to fully blossom, I found solace in the notion that my circumstances had improved since severing ties with Irvin. While I still indulged in marijuana alongside Shelly, Victor, and our newfound friend Kassidy, I had managed to distance myself from the grip of methamphetamine addiction. Focused on reclaiming autonomy and stability, I channeled my earnings toward saving for a future of independence, amassing a modest sum of $1,000.

Gratitude overflowed within me for Shelly and Victor's unwavering support during my darkest hours. In a gesture of appreciation, I extended a helping hand, offering to purchase diapers and formula for their child, treating them to shopping sprees, and stocking our humble abode with groceries and food, despite my own limited consumption. Sacrificing privacy and comfort, I willingly contributed to the household expenses, even if it meant sleeping on a mattress in the crowded living room. It was a decision fueled by gratitude and a desire to repay the kindness bestowed upon me, yet one tinged with the hindsight realization of its folly.

Foolishness is bound up in the heart of a child;
The rod of discipline will remove it far from him.
Proverbs 22:15 NASB

My journey is a testament to the transformative power of faith and the unwavering grace of the Lord. Through trials and tribulations, I have emerged with a profound understanding of the lessons imparted by divine discipline, and my gratitude for His guidance shines brightly. In the midst of the strip club environment, I steadfastly held onto God's principles, recognizing the job for what it was—a means of earning a living. While many succumbed to the allure of a superficial lifestyle, I was able to remain grounded, refusing to compromise my values by indulging in scanty attire, excessive makeup, or a superficial attitude. Instead, I embraced my role as a beacon of light, offering solace and prayer to fellow dancers grappling with their own troubles. My compassion and strength earned me the title of "House Mom," a testament to my nurturing spirit and unwavering resolve.

Despite the allure of easy money and illicit activities, I remained resolute in my commitment to righteousness, steadfastly refusing to engage in sexual acts for financial gain. My steadfast refusal to compromise my integrity is a testament to my unwavering faith and the transformative power of God's grace. My story serves as a powerful testament to the resilience of the human spirit and the redemptive power of faith. By staying true to my beliefs and trusting in the Lord's guidance, I have emerged stronger, wiser, and filled with gratitude for the journey that has brought you closer to His divine light.

The journey to independence and self-reliance is often fraught with challenges and moments of uncertainty. Despite my resilience and determination, I encountered frightening incidents that served as stark reminders of the dangers lurking in the shadows. There was an encounter with a taxi driver and a suspicious follower which underscored the precarious nature of my circumstances, highlighting the importance of vigilance and seeking safety in times of peril. The swift action taken by the taxi driver to return me to the club exemplifies the power of intuition and the willingness of others to protect those in need.

Furthermore, there was an unsettling encounter with a woman at the club during my day shift that evoked a sense of unease and apprehension. She introduced herself as Sally and mentioned she was a friend of Irvin's, which sent a chill down my spine, prompting a heightened sense of caution and concern. Fearful of the potential repercussions, I took proactive measures to safeguard myself, alerting the bar staff to the possibility of Irvin's presence and instructing them to notify me immediately if he appeared.

In the face of adversity, my resilience and resourcefulness shone through, as I navigated the complexities of my circumstances with unwavering determination and grace. My willingness to confront the unknown head-on and take decisive action to protect myself is a testament to the strength and courage of God within me.

Before long, Sally returned to the club, claiming to audition as a dancer. Her proximity and attempts at familiarity stirred a sense of unease within me, particularly when she handed me her phone. I was greeted by

Irvin's voice on the other end. Swiftly disconnecting the call, I recoiled from the unwanted intrusion, recognizing the insidious presence of my past once more.

As my shift drew to a close, the unwelcome sight of Irvin sent a shiver down my spine. Despite his attempts to engage me in conversation, I remained steadfast, refusing to acknowledge his presence or entertain his pleas. Sally's misguided attempts to meddle in my affairs only served to exacerbate the tension, as she implored me to reconsider giving Irvin another chance. Resolute in my decision to distance myself from Irvin's toxic influence, I rebuffed Sally's interference with a firm yet polite refusal, asserting my boundaries and asserting my independence. Yet, in a moment of vulnerability, I made the ill-fated decision to accept a ride home from Sally's boyfriend, a choice born of misplaced trust and a desire for convenience.It was a stark reminder of the dangers of letting down one's guard in the face of familiarity, and the importance of remaining vigilant and steadfast in the pursuit of one's safety and well-being.

The deceptive act orchestrated by Sally and her boyfriend left me feeling trapped and vulnerable, a pawn in their cruel game. Despite the sinking feeling in my gut, I summoned the courage to gather my belongings and prepare to leave. However, Irvin's sudden appearance thwarted my escape, drawing me into an unwanted encounter.

Reluctantly, I followed him to his new apartment, a stark departure from the cluttered and chaotic environment I remembered from before. As I stepped inside, the cleanliness and orderliness of the space struck me, a stark contrast to the disarray of my memories. Irvin's offer of refreshments was met with a polite refusal as I braced myself for the conversation ahead. His words, tinged with remorse and self-reflection, echoed in the stillness of the room. Irvin's admission of foolishness and repentance for his past behavior rang with a sincerity that caught me off guard. His assurances of a newfound path away from drugs and crime, accompanied by promises of change and redemption, stirred conflicting emotions within me.

Caught between skepticism and a flicker of hope, I grappled with the weight of his words, torn between the desire for closure and the fear of falling back into old patterns. In this moment of vulnerability, I stood at a crossroads, uncertain of the path that lay ahead, yet steadfast in my resolve to prioritize my own well-being above all else.

As I entered Irvin's new apartment, the pristine cleanliness of the space contrasted sharply with the chaotic memories of our past. Despite my initial resistance, I found myself drawn into a conversation with him, his words dripping with remorse and self-reflection. Irvin's sincerity tugged at my heartstrings, stirring a maelstrom of conflicting emotions within me.

His professed desire for change and redemption ignited a flicker of hope within me, a yearning for closure and a chance at reconciliation. Yet, beneath the surface, a nagging skepticism lingered, whispering warnings of past betrayals and broken promises. Caught in the throes of uncertainty, I grappled with the weight of my decision, torn between the allure of a second chance and the fear of repeating past mistakes. In the end, I knew that my journey to healing and wholeness could not be contingent upon Irvin's promises alone. With a heavy heart, I resolved to prioritize my own well-being above all else, steeling myself against the temptation to veer off course once more. As I bid farewell to Irvin and his apartment, I stepped into the unknown with a renewed sense of purpose, determined to forge a path forward guided by faith, resilience, and the unwavering grace of God.

For God is not a God of confusion but of peace.
1 Corinthians 14:33 ESV

The internal struggle between the yearning for reconciliation and the wariness of past hurts weighed heavily on my mind as I grappled with the decision of whether to reach out to Irvin once more. Despite my reservations, the allure of familiarity and the hope for a brighter future clouded my judgment, leading me to extend an olive branch in the form of a dinner invitation. As I entered Irvin's home that evening, my guard remained firmly in place, wary of the potential for disappointment and betrayal. To my surprise, Irvin's demeanor was unexpectedly polite and respectful, offering a glimmer of reassurance amidst the uncertainty.

Irvin pleaded with me for another chance, stirring in me a sense of guilt and obligation. In a moment of weakness, I agreed to give our relationship another try. But the next morning, as morning light filtered through the curtains, the weight of this decision pressed upon me once more. With a heavy heart, I turned to Shelly and Victor, my steadfast allies in times of turmoil, to share my decision. Despite their reservations, they offered their understanding, albeit tinged with concern for my well-being. As the days passed and the time drew near for my departure, I left Shelly and Victor with my share of the rent before embarking on a new chapter with Irvin. Yet, beneath the facade of optimism lay a lingering sense of apprehension, a nagging doubt that whispered of the perils lurking on the horizon.

In the face of uncertainty, I clung to the fragile hope that love and forgiveness would pave the way to redemption, praying that this time, things would be different.

The initial euphoria of a seemingly fresh start with Irvin gradually gave way to a tumultuous whirlwind of emotions as his unexpected proposal left me reeling. Caught off guard by the suddenness of his request, I accepted. Immediately, though, I grappled with a surge of uncertainty and apprehension, questioning the wisdom of such a monumental decision.

Despite my initial reservations, I found myself swept up in Irvin's enthusiasm and the whirlwind of wedding preparations that ensued. As I immersed myself in the frenetic pace of dance performances to finance our impending nuptials, I unwittingly became entangled in a web of expectations and obligations.

Irvin's efforts to orchestrate the perfect wedding, with the assistance of his mother Greta and his circle of friends, only served to compound my unease. His eagerness to involve my father, despite their lack of prior acquaintance, underscored the gravity of the situation and the weight of familial expectations. In my desperation for stability and belonging, I allowed myself to be swept along by the tide of events, oblivious to the warning signs that lurked beneath the surface.

Little did I know that my acceptance would herald the beginning of a tumultuous journey fraught with challenges and heartache. The shadows of the past loomed ever closer, threatening to shatter the fragile facade of happiness I had so fervently sought. The eve of our wedding should have been filled with anticipation and joy, but instead, it was marred by a revelation that shattered the fragile illusion of happiness I had clung to. As Pete,

Irvin's best man-to-be, entered our home bearing a sinister gift, my unease transformed into outright horror.

The offer of crystal meth, made in the sanctity of our own space, laid bare the deception that had clouded our relationship. In that moment of reckoning, the truth emerged, cruel and unforgiving—Irvin's supposed reformation was nothing more than a facade, a charade designed to deceive me into believing in a fantasy.

I stood at a crossroads, faced with a choice that would shape the trajectory of my life. The allure of escapism beckoned, promising temporary relief from the crushing weight of reality. In a moment of weakness and desperation, I succumbed to the siren song of addiction, forsaking my principles in a bid to salvage the shattered remnants of our union.

The days that followed were a blur of self-destructive behavior and agonizing regret, as I descended further into the depths of addiction alongside Irvin and Pete. What should have been a joyous occasion transformed into a nightmare, a cruel twist of fate that condemned me to a cycle of despair and disillusionment that would span nearly a decade.

In the shadow of betrayal and broken promises, I embarked on a journey fraught with darkness and despair, clinging to the faint hope that redemption lay on the distant horizon. Yet, as the years wore on, the echoes of that fateful night continued to haunt me, a grim reminder of the consequences of succumbing to temptation and forsaking the path of righteousness.

So, for one who knows the right thing to do
and does not do it, for him it is sin.
James 4:17 NASB

The first night of our marriage unfolded amidst a cacophony of chaos and despair, a stark juxtaposition to the dreams of blissful union that had once danced in my mind. As we crossed the threshold into our shared abode, the grim reality of our surroundings cast a pall over the nascent promise of our life together.

Above us, the raucous sounds of revelry echoed through the walls, a dissonant symphony that spoke volumes of the tumultuous lives unfolding in the apartments above. The air was thick with tension and unease, as if the very walls themselves bore witness to the secrets and sorrows of those who dwelled within.

As the night wore on, the veil of normalcy unraveled, revealing the unsettling truths that lurked beneath the surface. The sudden arrest of our next-door neighbor, the echoes of violence ringing in the stillness of the night, served as a grim reminder of the fragility of existence. Meanwhile, the solemn ritual of a neighbor mourning the loss of a beloved pet cast a somber shadow over the shared space between our yards. Amidst the chaos and uncertainty, I found myself grappling with the weight of disillusionment, the harsh reality of our circumstances serving as a stark reminder of the challenges that lie ahead. Yet, in the midst of the darkness, a glimmer of hope from God flickered within me, a testament to the resilience of the human spirit and the unwavering belief in the possibility of redemption amidst the ruins.

The fleeting illusion of marital bliss shattered with alarming swiftness as Irvin reverted to his old habits, plunging us back into the murky depths of addiction and chaos. The sanctity of our home was violated as a slew of druggie friends descended upon our apartment, their presence a stark reminder of the turbulent path we had chosen to tread.

One night, disoriented and weary from long hours of dancing, I returned home to find the apartment overrun with strangers, their hazy silhouettes a haunting echo of past indiscretions. With a heavy heart and a sense of resignation, I implored them to depart, their lingering presence a disruptive force in the fragile tranquility of our shared space.

Yet, even as I sought refuge in the solace of sleep, the specter of uncertainty loomed large, casting a shadow over the fragile facade of normalcy. In the silence of the night, I found myself grappling with the harsh reality of our circumstances, a poignant reminder of the tumultuous journey that lay ahead.

Irvin was angry that I asked them to leave, so he dragged me into the bedroom by my hair and punched me in the face until I was bloody. He locked me in the bedroom so no one would see what he had done.

This was just the beginning of a miserable life. I became even more depressed than before, and I continued dancing and doing meth with Irvin, getting beaten almost every day. I left a few times to find resources for women in domestic violence situations. I found one place and even called to register for an open bed, but somehow Irvin found out and I did not go. There were a few times that the police showed up at our apartment for a call about domestic violence. Just about two years after we were married–I was 27–the police separated us to talk to us individually, and I told them that he punched me in the face. The police ended up taking him to jail for domestic abuse and a probation violation because they had found a meth pipe on him and were aware of his drug and assault charges from about four years ago.

In a moment of vulnerability and fear, I reached out to Irvin's mother, Greta, seeking solace and refuge from the chaos that engulfed our apartment. With trembling hands and a heavy heart, I recounted the unsettling events that had transpired, the specter of isolation looming large in the recesses of my mind. In a gesture of maternal concern, Greta offered her support and reassurance, promising to whisk me away from the turmoil and provide sanctuary in the safety of her home. With gratitude and relief coursing through my veins, I accepted her offer, clinging to the lifeline she extended amidst the storm.

As the night descended and the neon lights of the club dimmed, Greta and her husband, Alan, arrived to ferry me away from the tumult of the city streets. With a sense of trepidation and anticipation, I gathered my belongings and embarked on a journey into the unknown, guided by the flickering beacon of familial love and understanding.

As we drove through the darkness, the weight of the night's events slowly began to lift, replaced by a glimmer of hope and the promise of respite in the embrace of loved ones. In that fleeting moment of transition, I found solace in the knowledge that, amidst the chaos and uncertainty, there existed a sanctuary of warmth and comfort on the horizon.

As we made our way to their place, the headlights pierced through the darkness, illuminating the road ahead. Suddenly, a car emerged from around a bend, seemingly out of nowhere, directly in our path. Panic surged as we realized there was no time to react. The impact was deafening, and we were jolted violently as our truck collided with the car. Shock gripped me as I fretted over the occupants of the other vehicle.

Alan's voice broke through the chaos, urging me to exit the truck and find refuge on the roadside with Greta until help arrived. Time seemed to stretch endlessly until the paramedics finally arrived, their arrival signaling the end of the harrowing night. We eventually made it to their home, seeking solace in sleep.

The following morning, I awoke to a world of agony, the daylight filtering through the curtains offering no relief. Irvin's presence beside me was a comforting anchor amidst the pain–Greta and Alan had already retrieved him from jail. Something felt dreadfully amiss as I struggled against the pain coursing through my body, especially my left collarbone. With Greta's recommendation, I found myself in the care of a compassionate chiropractor, who shed light on the extent of my injuries: a dislocated collarbone, mild scoliosis, and a bulging disc in my neck.

The incident served as a clear indication that I needed to take a step back from dancing, allowing my body the time it needed to heal. For three long months, I adhered to a regimen of rest and regular chiropractic sessions, gradually witnessing improvements in my condition. Feeling optimistic about my progress, I made the decision to return to the club, albeit with caution. Taking on light dancing duties, I aimed to supplement our income, supporting both Irvin and me as we navigated through this challenging time.

The next several years consisted of meth use, verbal, physical, emotional, psychological, and sexual abuse. In 2008, a troubling incident unfolded when Irvin committed theft at a department store, discreetly slipping stolen DVDs into my purse. Both of us found ourselves in the grip of the law, detained and subsequently released by the police, and burdened with fines for the charge of theft in the third degree. Shockingly, a similar scenario unfolded in 2009, leading to identical repercussions.

Amidst the turmoil of these events, a poignant moment emerged when I stumbled upon Ruthie's cherished Bible while unpacking boxes in our apartment. With Irvin absent, I seized the opportunity to delve into its sacred pages, immersing myself in its timeless wisdom. Lost in the Scriptures, I was oblivious to Irvin's return until he entered the bedroom, his eyes falling upon me engrossed in the holy text. Instantly, his demeanor shifted, consumed by a volatile anger at the sight of me embracing my grandmother's teachings.

He picked me up by the hair and threw me off of the bed, then grabbed my grandmother's Bible. I begged him to leave the Bible alone, but he took the Bible into our backyard and burned it right in front of me while I sobbed. Irvin said, "There is no God, and you cannot be saved, so don't ever let me catch you reading this trash again, or I will ****ing end you!"

Amidst the tumultuous trials that seemed to besiege my life, I couldn't ignore the nagging feeling that these events were God's interventions, guiding me to reassess the path I had chosen in marrying Irvin. Despite the unmistakable signs and the overwhelming sense of misery that shrouded me, I stubbornly persisted in my marriage. One fateful day, as I trudged home from the grocery store burdened with both bags of groceries and the weight of my inner turmoil, I passed by a beckoning church. A desperate impulse seized me, prompting me to step inside, seeking solace and clarity amidst the pews. Wrestling with the agonizing decision of whether to endure the abuse within my marriage or to take the daunting step towards divorce, I sought counsel from a figure who appeared to be the pastor.

With a heavy heart, I poured out my innermost struggles to him, hoping for a glimmer of guidance in the darkness that engulfed me. His response, laden with the weight of religious doctrine, echoed through the hallowed halls of the church, urging me to uphold my marital vows and endeavor to lead my husband towards salvation, even in the face of adversity. Yet, the conflict within me deepened; I was torn between the dictates of faith and the urgent call for self-preservation.

> *Jesus replied, "Every plant not planted*
> *by my heavenly Father will be uprooted,*
> *so ignore them.*
> *They are blind guides,*
> *and if one blind person guides another,*
> *they will both fall into a ditch."*
> **Matthew 15:13-14 NLT**

Despite my wavering faith and inner turmoil, I succumbed to the pastor's counsel, clinging to the hope that perseverance and kindness would eventually mend the fractures in our tumultuous marriage. But as time wore on, it became painfully clear that my efforts were in vain. Irvin's treatment of me grew no less abusive, and our relationship remained ensnared in dysfunction.

In a bid for a fresh start, we relocated to a different apartment across town, where I resolved to leave behind my previous life as a dancer and seek other employment. However, every job opportunity I pursued was sabotaged by Irvin's interference, leaving me stranded without means of financial independence. With no other recourse, we relied solely on Irvin's Social Security benefits to sustain us in the ensuing years. Amidst the suffocating confines of our dysfunctional existence, I retreated to the sanctuary of our closet with a flashlight and the pocket Bible I had hidden away. In the dim glow of the flashlight, I found fleeting comfort within the sacred verses, a beacon of hope in the midst of my darkest hours.

Irvin found me reading again and dragged me out of the closet by my hair and punched me as I fell to the ground. He took the small Bible, held it over the toilet, and burned it as he did the last one. Despite enduring Irvin's harsh mistreatment, a glimmer of determination flickered within me, fueled by a shared conviction with his mother, Greta. Together, we embarked on a mission to steer Irvin towards a legitimate and lawful path in his passion for tattooing. Over the course of ten arduous months, I stood steadfast by his side, offering unwavering support as he pursued his education. From assisting him in his studies to preparing his daily lunches and ensuring he made it to the bus stop on time, I spared no effort in facilitating his journey. Each day, I accompanied him on his commute, greeting him at the end of his school day with a reassuring smile.

As Irvin advanced in his training, I made a pivotal decision to offer myself as a canvas for his practice tattoo work. Through the pain and permanence of the ink etched into my skin, I silently bore witness to the transformation taking place within Irvin, hopeful that this newfound sense of purpose would herald a brighter future for us both. In the waning months of 2011, marking the fifth year of our tumultuous union and coinciding with my milestone 30th birthday, we found a new apartment nestled in a supposedly safer corner of town. Despite the outward change in scenery, the shadows of dysfunction and abuse persisted, casting a pall over our fragile marriage.

Caught in the grip of substance abuse, I found myself in a cycle of methamphetamine and marijuana use, locked in a dangerous dance with

Irvin that offered fleeting moments of euphoria amidst the turmoil. Blinded by a false sense of self-fulfillment, I remained oblivious to the lurking perils that loomed on the horizon, ensnared in a web of complacency that threatened to engulf me whole.

I recall the quiet moments of prayer, my whispered pleas rising to the heavens, seeking God's intervention in our lives. It was a time when I believed that the arrival of a child might be the catalyst for Irvin's spiritual awakening. But reality veered sharply from my hopes. In the early months of 2012, a subtle shift in my body prompted me to take a pregnancy test. Hope surged as the test confirmed my suspicions, but Irvin's subdued reaction cast a shadow over my joy. That day, the world crumbled around me as a second test revealed a different truth—one of loss and devastation. The confirmation from medical professionals only deepened the ache within me.In the echo of grief, I continued to pour out my soul in prayer, sharing my anguish and unfulfilled longing with God. Through the hushed whispers of my soul, I sought understanding, seeking guidance on the path ahead. And in the stillness, the Holy Spirit whispered back, urging me to embrace a different way of living. As the waning days of 2012 faded into the dawn of a new year, I made a solemn vow—a pledge to forsake the tumultuous lifestyle that had ensnared Irvin and me.

Resolved firmly in my heart, I turned away from the allure of drugs, the haze of cigarette smoke, and the numbing embrace of alcohol. It was a decision rooted in self-respect, a declaration of autonomy over my body and soul. And in that pivotal moment of transformation, I began to tread a path illuminated by faith and fortitude, trusting in God's guiding hand to lead me toward a future filled with hope and purpose.

One night, as the evening shadows lengthened and Irvin returned home, a familiar sense of apprehension tinged the air. I watched in silence as he busied himself with the paraphernalia of his destructive habit, the metallic glint of a lighter casting ominous shadows across the room. With a resolve born of newfound conviction, I summoned the courage to confront the looming specter of addiction. "I've made a decision," I announced, my voice steady despite the tremor of uncertainty that lingered within. "I no longer wish to partake in this lifestyle. I refuse to continue down this path of self-destruction."

Irvin's response was a mixture of indifference and scorn, his laughter a harsh echo of derision. "Figures," he sneered, his words laced with mockery. "Always the goody two-shoes."

Yet, in that moment of confrontation, I found an unexpected strength —an unyielding resolve tempered by the unwavering faith that had sustained me through trials and tribulations. His taunts, once potent arrows that pierced the armor of my confidence, now fell impotent against the shield of my determination. And as the echoes of his ridicule faded into the silence of the night, I stood firm in my resolve, emboldened by the knowledge that I was no longer bound by the chains of addiction, but guided by the unwavering light of faith.

Amidst the solitude of Irvin's absence, I found solace in the quiet moments of introspection and reflection. One afternoon, as the sun cast its golden hues upon the streets outside our apartment, I embarked on a solitary journey to the nearby grocery store. The familiar faces of the store's employees greeted me warmly, their genuine smiles a balm to the wounds of loneliness. Among them stood Alyssen, a beacon of kindness amidst the chaos of my turbulent life. In the hallowed aisles of the grocery store, we forged an unexpected bond—one forged in the shared language of faith and compassion. I confided in her the harrowing truth of my existence, the shadows of abuse looming large in the corners of my existence.

With gentle words and fervent prayers, Alyssen offered me a lifeline— a pocket-sized testament to the power of faith and resilience. As she pressed the worn pages of her cherished Bible into my trembling hands, I felt a surge of gratitude wash over me, a tide of hope amidst the wreckage of despair.

In that simple act of generosity, Alyssen became more than a mere acquaintance. Through her selfless gesture, she not only bestowed upon me the gift of her Bible but also ignited within me the flickering flames of a newfound relationship with God—a beacon of hope that would illuminate the darkest corners of my soul.

He who is gracious and lends a hand to the poor
lends to the LORD.
And the LORD will repay him for his good deed.
Proverbs 19:17 AMP

Immersed in the sacred verses of Alyssen's Bible, I found solace and strength in the whispered promises of divine guidance. Day by day, as I delved deeper into its pages, I fervently prayed for God's Word to manifest itself in my life, to illuminate the path toward healing and redemption.

As Irvin's erratic behavior continued to cast its dark shadow over our home, I found myself strangely immune to his verbal barbs. Instead of succumbing to the familiar sting of his insults, I turned my gaze heavenward, beseeching God to intercede in his troubled heart, to free us both from the shackles of abuse.

Yet, it was a moment of unexpected vulnerability that crystallized my awakening. As I tended to Irvin in an hour of sickness, his fevered words cutting through the silence like jagged shards of glass, I felt a stirring within me—a realization as profound as it was unsettling.

In the gentle glow of the bedside lamp, as I wiped the sweat from his brow and soothed his trembling form, I came face to face with a truth I had long denied: the embers of romantic love that once burned brightly had dwindled to mere ashes. And though I had never dared utter the words aloud, I knew in that moment that the bonds of affection that had once bound us were now but fragile threads, frayed and worn by the weight of our shared turmoil.

Amidst the whirlwind of emotions that accompanied the fact that for the second time I found out that I was going to be a mother, a glimmer of hope illuminated the shadows of uncertainty that had long haunted our home. With each passing day, the swell of anticipation grew, a testament to the miraculous journey unfolding within me.

Yet, as the weeks turned into months, Irvin's absence became a familiar refrain—I was a solitary figure in a landscape marked by longing and solitude. Though his words spoke of joy and anticipation, his actions told a different tale—a tale woven with threads of neglect and indifference. In the quiet of our shared space, I navigated the uncharted waters of pregnancy with a mixture of trepidation and quiet resolve. Days blurred into one another, punctuated only by Irvin's sporadic presence—a presence marked by volatility and unrest.

And then, in a moment of unbridled fury, the tenuous facade of tranquility shattered, giving way to a storm of violence and fear. With the safety of my unborn child paramount in my mind, I fled, seeking refuge in the sanctuary of a nearby park—a haven of solace amidst the chaos of my reality. With each whispered prayer and tear-stained page of my Bible, I beseeched the heavens for deliverance, for the strength to break free from the chains of abuse that ensnared me. And though the path ahead remained shrouded in uncertainty, I clung to the unwavering promise of divine intervention, trusting in God to forge a path to freedom and redemption.

One day, during a daily walk,, a sudden rupture heralded the imminent arrival of new life. With a mixture of excitement and apprehension, I reached out to Irvin, the tether that bound me to the world beyond. Together, we embarked on a journey to the hospital, propelled by the promise of impending parenthood. As the wheels of his mother's car carried us through the quiet streets, I felt a sense of calm settle over me, a quiet assurance that, for once, Irvin would remain by my side. And true to his word, he stood steadfast beside me as the minutes stretched into hours, each passing moment a testament to the bond that held us together.

And then, in a flurry of anticipation and pain, the moment arrived—a moment that would forever alter the course of our lives. With each passing hour, the veil between worlds grew thinner, until finally, after 32 arduous hours, the cries of new life pierced the air, heralding the arrival of our son, Peter. In the hushed embrace of the hospital room, I cradled my newborn son in trembling arms, marveling at the fragile beauty of his existence. And as the days slipped by in a blur of exhaustion and wonder, I remained ensconced within the sanctuary of the hospital walls, cocooned in the warmth of maternal love and the reassuring hum of medical care.

For three days and nights, I lingered in that liminal space between past and future, between pain and joy, until finally, with the gentle reassurance of doctors and nurses alike, I emerged into the dawn of a new day—a day filled with promise and possibility, anchored by the love that bound us together as a family.

In the quiet moments of early motherhood, as the days blurred into nights and the routine of caring for Peter became my world, a subtle shift unfolded—a shift marked by the gradual transition from breast to bottle, from the intimacy of nursing to the practicality of formula and pumped milk. Though the change brought its own set of challenges, I embraced it with the same quiet resolve that had carried me through the trials of childbirth.

Yet, amidst the tender moments of bonding with my newborn son, a shadow loomed on the horizon—a shadow cast by Irvin's prolonged absences, his days consumed by the demands of his profession. Day after day, he vanished into the recesses of the tattoo shop, leaving me to navigate the unfamiliar terrain of parenthood alone. And then, amidst the monotony of routine, an unexpected opportunity presented itself—a chance to immortalize the bond between mother and child in the vibrant hues of ink. With Irvin's skillful hands poised to etch Peter's name onto my skin, I eagerly embraced the prospect of a tangible reminder of our shared journey.

Yet, as the needle traced its intricate patterns across my skin, an unwelcome presence intruded upon the sanctity of the moment. A woman named Stephanie entered the tattoo shop, her dark hair cascading like a veil around her shoulders, her familiarity with Irvin casting a pall over the room. In the glances and whispered conversations, I sensed the specter of betrayal lurking in the shadows, a silent witness to the erosion of trust that had long sustained our marriage. And though the truth remained unspoken, a palpable tension hung heavy in the air—a silent testament to the fractures that had begun to form within the fragile confines of our once-unbreakable bond. And as we made our way home in the fading light of evening, the weight of unspoken truths bore down upon me, a burden too heavy to bear alone.

One day, in the hushed confines of our home, the air thick with the weight of unspoken truths, a sudden intrusion shattered the fragile tranquility of the moment. Irvin and Greta arrived together, sending tremors of unease coursing through my veins. As Greta whisked Peter away into the gathering dusk, a sense of foreboding settled over me, a silent premonition of the storm that loomed on the horizon. And then, in the stark silence that followed, Irvin confessed his infidelity, a betrayal that cut deeper than any blade.

With trembling hands and a heart heavy with sorrow, I confronted the truth that lay bare before me—a truth obscured by the shadows of deceit. And as the weight of Irvin's admission bore down upon me, I felt a tumult of emotions rise within me—a tempest of anger, hurt, and betrayal swirling within the depths of my soul.

In the dim light of a fading day, I stood before him, my words a whispered echo of the pain that consumed me. And though his gaze remained fixed upon the ground, I knew that the bond that had once bound us had been irreparably broken—a bond shattered by the jagged edges of his deception. And so, with a heavy heart and a voice choked with emotion, I bid him farewell—a farewell tinged with the bitter taste of betrayal, a farewell that marked the end of a chapter in our shared history. And as he turned to leave, the echoes of my words lingered in the air—a silent plea for healing, for closure, for the faint glimmer of hope that lay beyond the darkness of our shattered dreams.

In the depths of despair, as the weight of betrayal and heartache pressed down upon me, I found myself adrift in a sea of tumultuous emotions—a whirlwind of anger, sorrow, and profound disillusionment. With each sob that wracked my body, I felt the tendrils of grief entwine themselves around my soul, dragging me deeper into the abyss of despair.

Yet, amidst the chaos of my shattered world, a flicker of God's illumination pierced the darkness—a revelation born from the pages of my Bible, a truth that cut through the layers of pain and confusion like a beacon in the night. In that sacred moment of clarity, I came face to face with the stark reality of my own misplaced devotion—a devotion that had unwittingly supplanted the divine with the flawed and fallible. With tears streaming down my cheeks, I cried out to the heavens, a broken plea for forgiveness, for redemption, and for the grace of a merciful God. And in the midst of my anguish, a profound transformation took root—a transformation that would shape the course of my life for eternity.

In that solemn vow of surrender, I relinquished the idols of my past—the false gods that had held sway over my heart—and embraced a newfound commitment to follow Christ, to walk in the light of His love and grace. And though the path ahead was fraught with uncertainty and sacrifice, I knew that with God by my side, I would find the strength to persevere, to overcome, to live a life worthy of His calling. So, with trembling hands and a heart ablaze with newfound faith, I bowed my head in prayer, surrendering myself to the divine will of the One who had loved me with an unfailing love—a love that would carry me through the darkest valleys and lead me into the glorious light of His eternal embrace.

"Have I not commanded you?
Be strong and courageous.
Do not be afraid;
do not be discouraged,
for the LORD your God
will be with you wherever you go."
Joshua 1:9 NIV

Chapter Seven

THE THREEFOLD CORD

As my 34th birthday in 2015 loomed closer, the weight of recent events pressed heavily upon me. Just days earlier, Irvin had handed me divorce papers, his words echoing with finality–he believed our marriage was irreparable. It was an answer to a prayer I had whispered in desperation, a plea for a way out of a union that had long been fractured. Yet, as I held those papers in my trembling hands, I found myself clinging to a semblance of hope for our relationship, a reluctance to let go of what I knew deep down was no longer meant for me. In that moment of confrontation, I tried to convince myself that forgiveness and reconciliation were still possible, that our love could withstand the storm of betrayal. But Irvin's admission cut through my denial like a sharp knife, his words a painful reminder of the reality I had been avoiding. Alone with my thoughts, I sought reassurance from God, a confirmation that letting go was indeed the path I needed to walk.

With a heavy but determined heart, I raised my hands in surrender, a silent acknowledgment of His guidance. "Okay, God," I whispered, my voice trembling with a mixture of fear and relief. "Please forgive my stubbornness. I surrender." In that moment of submission, I felt a weight lift from my shoulders, a sense of liberation washing over me like a gentle tide. With a pen in hand, I hesitated only briefly before signing the divorce papers, each stroke of ink symbolizing the release of years of pain and uncertainty. "Thank You," I murmured softly, my words a grateful echo of newfound freedom. As I embraced the truth that had eluded me for so long, a sense of peace settled within me, a quiet assurance that I was finally on the path I was meant to walk. And in that sacred moment of acceptance, the threads of faith, hope, and courage intertwined within me, weaving a threefold cord that would guide me forward into the unknown.

"And you will know the truth,
and the truth will set you free."
John 8:32 NLT

As Irvin and I sat side by side in the stark office of the courthouse, the weight of our decision hung heavy in the air. With the help of the family law representative, we navigated the maze of paperwork, our signatures marking the end of a chapter we had once hoped would last a lifetime. Despite the pain and disappointment that lingered between us, there was a shared understanding, a mutual agreement to prioritize the well-being of our son above all else. We settled on joint custody, a decision reached with a sense of reluctant compromise. Irvin's commitment to provide financial support, though meager, was a small gesture of responsibility in the wake of his departure. With each document signed and filed away, the finality of our divorce loomed closer, a bittersweet resolution to years of tumult and strife.

As the calendar turned to September 2015, marking the official beginning of a new chapter, the weight of freedom mingled with the burden of uncertainty. Life after divorce was a landscape fraught with challenges, a daunting journey through the aftermath of years spent in the shadows of abuse and neglect. Yet, amid the darkness, there was a glimmer of hope, a flicker of light beckoning me forward into the unknown.

With the keys to a new beginning firmly in hand, I stepped into the unfamiliar terrain of single parenthood, guided by a newfound sense of purpose and determination. Though the road ahead was fraught with obstacles, I knew I was no longer bound by the chains of my past. And so, with each passing day, I found refuge in the pages of the Bible, the words of scripture serving as a beacon of hope in the midst of uncertainty.

As I immersed myself in the teachings of Jesus, I felt a sense of peace wash over me, a reassurance that I was not alone in my journey. And as I read aloud to Peter, his innocent laughter echoing through the room, I knew that I was exactly where I was meant to be. Amidst the chaos of life's trials and tribulations, I clung to the promise of redemption, knowing that with faith as my guide, I could weather any storm that came my way.

> *I can do all things through Him who gives me strength.*
> **Philippians 4:13 NIV**

The Scripture that became my anchor during the darkest of days was **Psalm 46:1:** *God is our refuge and strength, an ever-present help in trouble.* In moments when doubt and despair threatened to consume me, these words served as a lifeline, a reminder that I was never alone in my struggles. With each verse etched into my heart, I found solace in the knowledge that God's guidance was ever-present, guiding me through the tumultuous waters of life's trials.

On days when the weight of my burdens seemed too heavy to bear, I drew strength from the promise of God's unwavering presence. In the quiet moments of prayer and reflection, I felt His reassuring hand upon my shoulder, a gentle reminder that I was capable of overcoming even the greatest of obstacles. And as I faced each new challenge with renewed determination, I found comfort in the knowledge that I was not walking this path alone.

Through the highs and lows of my journey, I clung to the belief that God's love would see me through, a steadfast beacon of hope illuminating the darkest of nights. And as I forged ahead with unwavering faith, I discovered a newfound resilience within myself, a strength born from the realization that I was never truly alone. With each passing day, I embraced the promise of Psalm 46:1, finding refuge in the knowledge that God's strength would carry me through even the most difficult of times.

> *But the LORD stood by me and*
> *strengthened and empowered me,*
> *so that through me the (gospel) message*
> *might be fully proclaimed,*

and that all the Gentiles might hear it;
and I was rescued from the mouth of the lion.
2 Timothy 4:17 AMP

The days stretched long and arduous as I grappled with the daunting task of providing for Peter's basic needs with little to no income to speak of. Despite Irvin's sporadic contributions, which often fell short of what he had promised, the burden of financial responsibility weighed heavily on my shoulders. With each passing week, the uncertainty of how to make ends meet loomed large, casting a shadow of doubt over our already precarious situation.

In the face of adversity, I turned to the simple act of walking, a routine that offered both physical respite and a glimmer of hope. With Peter snug in his stroller, I traversed the familiar streets of our town, a silent witness to the ebb and flow of daily life. Armed with determination and resolve, I set out on a mission to collect cans, scouring alleyways and sidewalks in search of discarded treasures.

As the days turned into weeks, my efforts yielded modest returns, a humble collection of aluminum cans that held the promise of a meager reward. And so, each Friday, I made my way to the grocery store, my pockets jingling with the weight of my makeshift earnings. With a sense of pride and humility, I exchanged my bounty for a precious package of diapers, a small but essential provision for Peter's well-being. In addition to my resourcefulness in scavenging cans, I relied on government assistance programs like WIC and food stamps to supplement our meager income. With these lifelines in place, I was able to secure essentials such as formula, milk, and juice, ensuring that Peter's needs were met despite the challenges we faced.

Though the road ahead was fraught with uncertainty, I refused to succumb to despair. With each step I took, I was reminded of the resilience that lay within me, a strength born from the unwavering love I held for my son. And as I walked hand in hand with Peter, I found solace in the knowledge that, despite the hardships we endured, we were bound together by a bond that transcended the trials of this world.

Amidst the challenges of daily life, the local library became a sanctuary of solace and inspiration for Peter and me. Inside, the shelves were lined with a treasure trove of Christian self-help literature, each volume a beacon of hope in the darkness of our struggles. One book in particular captured my heart and mind, its title a promise of renewal and transformation: *The Power of Positive Thinking* by Norman Vincent Peale. Within its pages, I found refuge from the storms of life, discovering a wealth of practical wisdom and spiritual guidance to navigate the tumultuous waters of uncertainty.

As I immersed myself in Peale's teachings, I felt a shift within me, a gradual loosening of the grip that fear and despair had held over my heart. With each word I read, a newfound sense of hope blossomed within me, illuminating the path towards healing and wholeness. Through the power of positive thinking, I began to reshape my perspective, learning to see the world through the lens of faith and optimism. In the quiet moments of reflection that followed, I allowed myself to linger in the presence of God, meditating on His Word and the peaceful truths it contained. As I delved deeper into scripture, I felt His presence envelop me like a warm embrace, filling the empty spaces within my soul with a sense of peace and serenity.

In the midst of life's trials and tribulations, books like these became my faithful companions, guiding me through the darkest of days with words of encouragement and inspiration.

> *Summing it all up, friends,*
> *I'd say you'll do best by filling your minds*
> *and meditating on things true, noble, reputable,*
> *authentic, compelling, gracious—*
> *the best, not the worst;*
> *the beautiful, not the ugly;*
> *things to praise, not things to curse.*
> **Philippians 4:8 MSG**

The beginning of the divorce and custody arrangement, with Peter just a year old and the wounds of betrayal still fresh, marked a tumultuous chapter in my life. Irvin's decision to move in with Stephanie, the final woman in a string of infidelities, only added salt to the festering wounds of our broken relationship. Their apartment, mere blocks away from ours, served as a constant reminder of the shattered dreams and promises left in its wake.

On one particular occasion, Irvin requested that I bring Peter over to their place for a few hours. Reluctantly, I packed the essentials–diapers, clothes, and baby food–and set out with Peter in tow, his laughter a stark contrast to the tension that hung heavy in the air. As I knocked on the door, the muffled sounds of raised voices reached my ears, a harbinger of the confrontation that awaited me on the other side. When Irvin finally opened the door, I was met with a wave of hostility, his demeanor a reflection of the tumultuous emotions that simmered beneath the surface.

Summoning all the courage I could muster, I confronted Irvin about his rude and demanding behavior, refusing to be treated with anything less than respect. Yet, before I could utter another word, Stephanie emerged from the shadows, her presence a volatile spark igniting the powder keg of emotions that engulfed us. In a barrage of expletives and threats, Stephanie unleashed her fury upon me, her words a venomous assault on my already fragile sense of self. Despite the chaos that surrounded me, I remained steadfast in my resolve, calmly asserting that the hostile environment was no place for our son.

With Peter's well-being paramount in my mind, I made the difficult decision to walk away, vowing to return only when the storm had passed. As I retraced my steps homeward, Stephanie's screams echoed in the distance, a haunting reminder of the toxic dynamics that had torn our family apart. Though the road ahead was fraught with uncertainty, I refused to allow myself to be consumed by bitterness or resentment. With Peter by my side, I forged ahead with unwavering determination, guided by a mother's love and a fierce determination to protect my son from the storm that raged around us.

The tumultuous dynamics between Irvin and Stephanie cast a long shadow over my life, their turbulent relationship a constant source of stress and turmoil. Time and again, I found myself caught in the crossfire of their fiery disputes, forced to navigate the treacherous waters of their tumultuous love affair. One particular incident stands out amidst the chaos–the day Irvin came knocking on my door, seeking refuge from yet another explosive argument with Stephanie. Though my instincts urged me to turn him away, a flicker of compassion led me to grant him temporary shelter. But as the minutes stretched on, it became increasingly clear that I could not bear the weight of his burdens any longer. With a heavy heart, I gently but firmly urged him to face his demons and confront his troubles head-on.

Yet, even as I tried to maintain a semblance of neutrality, I found myself ensnared in Stephanie's web of rage and resentment. Her incessant phone calls, filled with threats of violence and aggression, served as a constant reminder of the toxicity that pervaded our lives. And though I refused to dignify her words with a response, the fear and anxiety they elicited lingered long after the calls had ended.

In the face of Stephanie's unwarranted animosity, I remained steadfast in my faith, drawing strength from the knowledge that I was not alone in my struggles. Though her actions spoke volumes of her own inner turmoil and spiritual emptiness, I refused to succumb to the darkness that threatened to engulf me. Instead, I chose to cling to the light of my faith, trusting in God to guide me through the storm. As I weathered the storms of Stephanie's wrath, I found solace in the unwavering love and support of those who stood by my side. And though the road ahead was fraught with uncertainty, I refused to allow fear or resentment to dictate my actions. For in the end, it was not hatred or violence that would prevail, but the enduring power of love and forgiveness.

> *But anyone who does not love*
> *does not know God,*
> *for God is love.*
> **1 John 4:8 NLT**

In the midst of my own feelings of anger and sadness, a gentle whisper stirred within my soul, urging me to rise above the bitterness and resentment that threatened to consume me. It was a voice I recognized all too well–the voice of God, beckoning me to embrace a higher calling, to extend grace and forgiveness where none seemed deserved.

With a heavy heart and trembling hands, I knelt in prayer, offering up petitions for the very individuals who had caused me so much pain. In those sacred moments of communion with the divine, I pleaded for Irvin and Stephanie to find redemption, to surrender their pride and selfish desires at the foot of the cross. As I lifted their names before the throne of grace, I felt a stirring of compassion within me, a recognition of our shared humanity and frailty. For despite the wounds they had inflicted upon me, I knew that they too were children of God, in need of His mercy and grace.

And so, day by day, I continued to intercede on their behalf, trusting in the transformative power of prayer to soften hearts and mend broken relationships. Though the road to reconciliation seemed long and arduous, I clung to the promise of divine intervention, knowing that God's love was greater than any obstacle we faced. In the act of praying for Irvin and Stephanie, I found healing for my own wounded soul, a release from the shackles of bitterness and resentment that had held me captive for so long. In extending forgiveness to others, I discovered the true meaning of grace–a gift freely given, yet infinitely precious in its ability to restore and renew. And as I lifted my voice in prayer, I entrusted their lives into the hands of a loving and merciful God, confident that He who had begun a good work in them would be faithful to complete it.

> *But I tell you, love your enemies*
> *and pray for those who persecute you.*
> **Matthew 5:44 NIV**

> *Humble yourselves, therefore,*
> *under God's mighty hand,*
> *that He may lift you up in due time.*
> **1 Peter 5:6 NIV**

Amidst the continued challenges and disappointments, I found solace in the quiet moments of reflection and prayer, surrendering my hurts and frustrations to God. Though Irvin and Stephanie's attitudes remained unchanged, I felt a shift within myself, a newfound sense of peace and resilience that transcended the turmoil surrounding me.

As I navigated the complexities of co-parenting with Irvin, I encountered moments of frustration and disappointment, each interaction a painful reminder of the brokenness that permeated our relationship. Yet, amidst the chaos, there were fleeting glimpses of cooperation and compromise, small gestures of goodwill that offered a glimmer of hope in the darkness. One such instance occurred when Irvin met me halfway between our homes to collect Peter for a few hours, a gesture of cooperation that spoke volumes of his willingness to put our son's needs above his own. However, these fleeting moments of civility were often overshadowed by the persistent challenges we faced as co-parents, leaving me to navigate the complexities of our relationship with a heavy heart.

A particularly troubling incident occurred when I visited Irvin and Stephanie's apartment to retrieve Peter, only to be met with an unsettling sight. The air was thick with the acrid scent of marijuana, and the apartment itself was in a state of disarray, cluttered and unkempt. Choosing to remain outside, I sensed a growing unease within me, a nagging suspicion that something was amiss.

Upon returning home with Peter, my worst fears were confirmed when I discovered telltale signs of bed bug bites on his delicate skin. With a heavy heart, I embarked on a relentless battle against the infestation, determined to protect my son from harm. Informing Irvin and Stephanie of the situation, I made it clear that Peter would not be returning to their apartment until the issue was resolved.

In the midst of this ordeal, I also observed concerning signs in Peter's development, prompting me to delve into research on autism spectrum disorder. Though met with skepticism from some medical professionals due to Peter's young age, I remained steadfast in my pursuit of answers, determined to ensure that my son received the support and care he needed. Despite the setbacks and challenges we faced, I refused to allow despair to overshadow my determination to provide Peter with the love and support he deserved. And as I weathered the storms of uncertainty, I clung to the hope that, with time and perseverance, we would emerge stronger and more resilient than ever before.

Amidst the turmoil and stress of living in close proximity to Irvin and Stephanie, a glimmer of hope emerged in the form of Greta's assistance in finding a new home for Peter and me. With her support, we discovered a duplex just five blocks away from Alan and Greta's place in another town, offering a much-needed respite from the constant tension and turmoil that had plagued our previous living arrangement.

The move brought a sense of relief, providing a welcome distance from the chaos of our past and offering a fresh start for Peter and me. Though the challenges of single parenthood remained ever-present, the newfound sense of peace and stability offered a ray of hope amidst the uncertainty of our circumstances.

One of the blessings of our new home was the opportunity to connect with Patricia, an early childhood development specialist who visited weekly to support Peter's growth and development. With her expertise and guidance, I gained valuable insights into Peter's unique needs and how best to support him on his journey. Patricia's dedication and genuine concern for Peter's well-being were a source of comfort and encouragement during those early days of single motherhood. Her presence in our lives served as a reminder that we were not alone in our struggles, that there were compassionate individuals willing to walk alongside us on our journey.

As Patricia worked tirelessly to support Peter's development, I felt a renewed sense of hope and optimism for the future. Though the road ahead would undoubtedly be challenging, I knew that with the support of caring individuals like Patricia, we would be able to navigate the complexities of single parenthood with grace and resilience. In the midst of uncertainty, I clung to the promise of brighter days ahead, trusting in the power of love and perseverance to guide us through the storms of life. And as Peter and I settled into our new home, surrounded by the love and support of friends and family, I felt a profound sense of gratitude for the blessings that had come our way.

The warmth of Patricia's friendship and support brought light and joy into our lives during a time of uncertainty and transition. Her unwavering dedication to Peter's well-being and her genuine kindness towards us both left an indelible mark on our hearts. As the weeks passed, Patricia's visits became more than just professional appointments; they became cherished moments of connection and camaraderie. Her genuine interest in Peter's growth and development extended beyond the confines of her role as a specialist, blossoming into a true friendship that enriched our lives in countless ways.

The bond between Patricia and Peter grew stronger with each passing day as they shared laughter, stories, and precious moments of joy together. And so, when Patricia and her family showed up on our doorstep on

Christmas Eve, bearing gifts and smiles, it felt like a small miracle. Their thoughtful gesture filled our hearts with warmth and gratitude, reminding us of the true spirit of the season—love, generosity, and the joy of giving.

As we gathered around the Christmas tree, exchanging gifts and laughter, I felt overwhelmed with gratitude for the friendship and support we had found in Patricia and her family. Their kindness and generosity were a testament to the power of community and the beauty of human connection. In Patricia, I had found not only a trusted ally and confidante, but also a cherished friend who had touched our lives in ways I could never have imagined. And as we celebrated the magic of Christmas together, surrounded by love and laughter, I knew that the bonds we had forged would endure long beyond the holiday season.

> *One who has unreliable friends soon comes to ruin,*
> *but there is a friend who sticks closer than a brother.*
> **Proverbs 18:24 NIV**

> *He who is gracious and lends a hand to the poor*
> *lends to the LORD,*
> *And the LORD will repay him for his good deed.*
> **Proverbs 19:17 AMP**

The unexpected visit from Mormon missionaries on Christmas Eve marked the beginning of a journey that would ultimately lead me down a path of discovery and enlightenment. Intrigued by their message of salvation through Jesus Christ, I welcomed them into my home with an open heart and mind, eager to explore the teachings of their faith.

As I attended services and delved deeper into the beliefs of the Mormon church, I found myself drawn to the sense of community and purpose it offered. The camaraderie of fellow believers and the promise of spiritual fulfillment were a beacon of hope in the midst of my own personal struggles. Yet, as I forged connections with other Christians, both in person and online, doubts began to creep in. Conversations with friends like Eli, whose deep understanding of religion shed light on the discrepancies between Mormon doctrine and Christian beliefs, left me questioning the foundation of my newfound faith.

As I delved deeper into research and introspection, I came to a sobering realization—that Mormonism, far from being the beacon of truth and salvation I had hoped for, was in fact a cult, steeped in secrecy and manipulation. The dark truths I uncovered about the manipulation between members shattered the illusion of spiritual enlightenment, leaving me disillusioned and betrayed. With a heavy heart and a sense of resolve, I made the difficult decision to sever ties with the Mormon church. Gathering my courage, I confronted the bishop with the truth of my discoveries, returning the Book of Mormon and demanding to be removed from their registry.

Though met with skepticism and resistance, I remained steadfast in my conviction, trusting in the voice of God to guide me on the right path. And as I walked away from the church that had promised salvation, I found solace in the knowledge that true faith was not found in the doctrines of men, but in the unwavering love and grace of Jesus Christ.

After I excused myself from the meeting with the bishop, I made a phone call to Utah's Mormon headquarters, insisting that mine and Peter's names be removed from the registry. Although our names were removed within two weeks' time, harassment from the Mormon church ensued, leaving me to call the police and have a harassment order placed on all church members!

Amidst the chaos and turmoil that surrounded me, a wave of mixed emotions crashed over me when Stephanie called. Despite the animosity that had existed between us, her tearful confession of abuse at the hands of Irvin stirred a sense of empathy and compassion within me.

As Stephanie poured out her heart, seeking guidance and solace in the midst of her own personal struggles, I found myself grappling with conflicting emotions. Though the wounds of our past interactions still lingered, I knew that beneath the facade of hostility lay a woman in desperate need of support and understanding. In that moment, I set aside my own hurt and resentment, offering Stephanie a listening ear and a word of encouragement. Though I could not dictate the path she should take, I assured her that she was not alone in her struggles, that there were people who cared about her well-being and were willing to offer a helping hand.

I urged Stephanie to prioritize her safety and well-being above all else, reminding her that she had the strength and resilience to overcome the challenges she faced. And as we parted ways, I made a solemn promise to lift her and Irvin up in prayer, trusting in the power of divine intervention to bring healing and restoration to their troubled relationship. In the midst of my own battles, I found solace in the act of extending grace and compassion to others, even those who had wronged me in the past. And as I navigated the complexities of forgiveness and reconciliation, I discovered the transformative power of love–a force capable of transcending even the deepest wounds and divisions.

But I say to you, love your enemies,
bless them that curse you,
do good to them that hate you,
and pray for those who spitefully use you
and persecute you.
Matthew 5:44 NKJV

Amidst the evolving dynamics of co-parenting with Irvin, I found myself grappling with a mix of emotions–from apprehension and concern to a profound sense of trust and surrender. As Irvin began to take a more active role in Peter's life, even initiating overnight visits, I was faced with the daunting task of entrusting my precious son into the care of someone whose lifestyle and choices filled me with unease.

In those quiet moments when Peter was away, I turned to prayer, seeking refuge in the arms of a loving and merciful God. With each whispered petition, I surrendered my fears and worries, placing Peter's well-being into the hands of the One who holds the universe in His grasp. Though doubts and concerns gnawed at my heart, I clung to the belief that God's watchful eye was upon Peter, guiding and protecting him even in the midst of uncertainty. And as I poured out my heart in prayer, I felt a sense of peace wash over me, a reassurance that transcended the turmoil of my circumstances.

Trusting in God's providence, I resolved to focus on the moments of joy and connection I shared with Peter, cherishing the precious time we had together and entrusting the rest to God's care. And though the road ahead remained fraught with challenges, I took comfort in the knowledge that I was not alone in my struggles but held firmly in the embrace of a loving and faithful God.

When Irvin returned with Peter, Irvin's behavior and Stephanie's state concerned me. I suspected they were intoxicated, and I felt a profound sense of urgency and responsibility weighing heavily on my heart. As I grappled with the decision of whether to involve Child Protective Services, I turned to prayer, seeking divine guidance and clarity in the face of uncertainty.

With each whispered plea, I laid my fears and doubts at the feet of a loving and compassionate God, trusting in His wisdom to illuminate the path forward. And as I waited for a sign, a confirmation that would validate my decision, I found myself attuned to the subtle whispers of His voice guiding me towards action. The following weekend, as Irvin once again arrived to take Peter home with him, the signs of intoxication were unmistakable. Stephanie's unconscious form slumped in the passenger seat. Irvin's disheveled appearance, slurred speech, and the faint scent of alcohol that lingered in his wake served as a chilling confirmation of the danger Peter faced in his care.

In that moment, I knew without a doubt that God had spoken, that this was the confirmation I had prayed for. With a heavy heart and a resolute determination, I made the difficult decision to reach out to Child Protective Services, trusting in the power of divine intervention to protect Peter from harm. Though the road ahead was fraught with uncertainty and challenges, I took solace in the knowledge that I had acted in accordance with God's will, seeking justice and protection for the innocent. And as I awaited the outcome of my decision, I held fast to the belief that God's hand was at work, guiding and protecting Peter every step of the way.

In the midst of the escalating turmoil and threats from Irvin, Stephanie, and even Irvin's mother Greta, I clung to my faith as a beacon of hope and strength in the face of adversity. Despite the fear and anxiety that threatened to overwhelm me, I turned to prayer as a source of comfort and guidance, entrusting my worries and fears into the hands of a loving and merciful God.

As I faced the fallout from my decision to involve Child Protective Services, I found myself grappling with a mix of emotions–from fear and uncertainty to a steadfast resolve to protect Peter from harm. Though the threats and hostility from Irvin, Stephanie, and Greta only served to deepen my sense of unease, I refused to be swayed from my course.

With each passing day, I drew strength from the knowledge that I was standing up for what was right, advocating for the safety and well-being of my son in the face of opposition and hostility. And though the road ahead was fraught with challenges, I remained steadfast in my faith, trusting in God's faithfulness to see us through even the darkest of times. In the midst of the storm, I clung to the promise of Psalm 23:4–"Even though I walk through the darkest valley, I will fear no evil, for you are with me; your rod and your staff, they comfort me." And as I navigated the treacherous waters of adversity, I found solace in the unwavering presence of a God who walked beside me every step of the way.

As the turmoil escalated, I felt overwhelmed and desperate. Eli, a good friend, prayed against the spiritual warfare raging. Meanwhile I was longing for respite from the constant barrage of hostility and harassment. Two other friends, Carrie and Doug, offered me sanctuary in their home. This offer, extended with open hearts and open arms, seemed like a beacon of hope in the midst of darkness.

With gratitude and relief, I accepted their offer, knowing that it would provide a much-needed reprieve from the chaos and turmoil that had engulfed my life. The prospect of a new beginning, far from the toxic environment that had plagued me for so long, filled me with a sense of renewed hope and determination. As I prepared to embark on this journey of healing and restoration, I felt a sense of peace wash over me, knowing that I was not alone, but surrounded by the love and support of friends who had become family in the midst of adversity.

Soon, however, what had seemed like a promising opportunity for refuge and stability devolved into a toxic environment filled with tension and hostility. An abrupt change in attitude of hostility from Carrie and Doug, coupled with the uncomfortable and unwelcome suggestion of intimacy in the form of sexual relations with them both, left me feeling deeply unsettled and disheartened.

As I confronted Carrie and Doug about their behavior, seeking answers to the sudden shift in dynamics, their silence only served to deepen my sense of disillusionment and disappointment. With a heavy heart, I realized that I could not subject myself and my son to such toxicity and negativity, even if it meant facing uncertainty once again. With a firm resolve, I made the difficult decision to seek alternative living arrangements for Peter and me, determined to find a safe and supportive environment where we could thrive free from the burden of hostility and animosity. Though the road ahead was fraught with challenges, I refused to allow fear or uncertainty to dictate my course of action, trusting instead in the guiding hand of divine providence to lead us to a place of peace and security.

As I embarked on this new chapter of our journey, I clung to the promise of Psalm 27:1–"The LORD is my light and my salvation; whom shall I fear? The LORD is the stronghold of my life; of whom shall I be afraid?" With faith as my compass and courage as my guide, I faced the unknown with a steadfast determination to forge a brighter future for myself and my son, confident in the knowledge that we were not alone, but held firmly in the embrace of a loving and faithful God.

Amidst the uncertainty and turmoil of seeking new living arrangements for Peter and me, I found myself grappling with a sense of desperation and apprehension. I turned to God in prayer, seeking His divine guidance and direction in the face of adversity. As I poured out my heart to God, He gently nudged me towards an unexpected solution–reaching out to my mother for help. Though hesitant and reluctant to rely on her assistance, I recognized the wisdom in His guidance. I swallowed my pride and made the call.

With a heavy heart, I recounted the events that had unfolded at Carrie and Doug's home, laying bare my vulnerability and need for support. Though my mother was hesitant, I knew that this was our best–and perhaps only–option for a safe and stable living environment. With a renewed sense of determination, I made arrangements for our move, enlisting the help of my brother Thomas and his wife Janice to assist us in relocating. Though the prospect of uprooting ourselves once again filled me with a sense of trepidation, I clung to the hope that this new chapter would bring us the peace and security we so desperately sought. As we embarked on this journey of transition and change, I knew God's guiding hand was at work, leading us towards a brighter future filled with hope and possibility. I faced the unknown with a steadfast resolve, trusting in His providence to see us through every step of the way.

In early 2018, Peter and I relocated to live with my mother. Without hesitation, I swiftly added our names to the county's housing waiting list, as we had lost our previous housing voucher due to moving counties. Concurrently, I pursued a spot for Peter on the waiting list of a reputable hospital nearby for his autism evaluation. Approximately two months later, my phone rang, and the hospital informed me of an appointment scheduled for Peter's autism evaluation. At just three and a half years old, Peter's journey towards understanding began.

The appointment confirmed what I had suspected: Peter indeed had autism along with a global developmental delay. With this diagnosis, I could finally initiate the process of applying for services, and that's precisely what I did. Making numerous phone calls, I tirelessly searched for a speech and occupational therapist suited for Peter's needs, along with an at-home care provider who could aid in his fine and gross motor development. It was an arduous journey finding the right fit, but eventually, I found a provider. They specialized in adult care and lacked experience with young children, but they were knowledgeable. Additionally, I enrolled Peter in Early Intervention Preschool services, aiming to foster his growth while honing his motor skills.

Throughout this challenging time, I leaned on the support of friends like Eli and the prayers offered by Pastor Barry from California. Their presence made life within my mother's household tolerable, as her behavior remained unchanged—she was still manipulative, verbally abusive, and controlling, rendering my living situation miserable. With the weight of responsibility on my shoulders, I realized it was time to seek employment again. Summoning courage, I broached the subject with my mother, asking if she could manage watching Peter while I worked part-time. Surprisingly, she agreed. Soon enough, I found a position at a local thrift store and spent seven months there. However, God had a different plan for me. A spinal injury from lifting heavy objects at work forced me to take a leave of absence, halting my employment journey abruptly.

Physically limited by my injury, my days were primarily consumed by chiropractic appointments, Peter's therapy sessions, and my own therapy sessions to address my mental health. Despite the pain, I managed to muster the strength to walk Peter to the bus for preschool and eagerly awaited his return home each day. During my moments of respite, Eli became a steadfast source of companionship and encouragement. Our conversations often revolved around our shared aspirations for further education, particularly through online avenues, given our roles as single parents of special needs children.

Motivated by our discussions, we embarked on a journey toward higher education, enrolling in the same online college program. Eli pursued a bachelor's degree in psychology, while I opted for an associate degree in early childhood education. Determined to make this endeavor possible, I spent some of my savings from tax returns on a laptop and internet service, essential tools for my studies. With Peter occupied at preschool, I dedicated my time to a routine of exercise and academic pursuits. The decision to pursue education brought a renewed sense of self-worth.

I gained additional financial stability when Peter's Social Security benefits were approved. With newfound confidence and a desire for independence, I set out to obtain my driver's license, a goal that necessitated the acquisition of a vehicle. I asked Thomas, a mechanic, to help me find a suitable car.

Accompanied by Thomas, I explored several cars within my budget, yet none met the standards of safety and reliability he deemed essential. However, a month later, Thomas reached out, informing me of a car he had acquired from his neighbor. Upon inspection, it proved to be a suitable choice, offering both quality and comfort. Encouraged by my newfound wheels, my mother generously offered to assist me in honing my driving skills, taking me out for practice sessions over the course of three months. With diligent preparation under my belt, I felt ready to tackle the driver's test. I approached the test with both nerves and determination, and to my elation, I passed on my first attempt!

The acquisition of my driver's license filled me with a sense of liberation, offering a reprieve from the oppressive atmosphere of my mother's home, which was characterized by bitterness and cold indifference. It marked the beginning of a new chapter, one filled with newfound freedom and independence.

Now, I could take Peter to his appointments myself, and this provided us both routine and a much-needed break from the confines of the house. However, one day after I had returned from an outing with Peter, my mother dropped a bombshell: she casually informed me that I'd need to consider moving out by the year's end. Her words sent a wave of anxiety coursing through me. Despite having saved some money from my job, it was far from sufficient to secure a new place, especially considering that my name had yet to surface on the housing list. The prospect of homelessness loomed ominously, a thought I couldn't bear, particularly with Peter's well-being at stake. Faced with uncertainty and desperation, I turned to prayer, once again seeking solace and guidance in God's Word.

Do not be anxious about anything,
but in every situation,
by prayer and petition with thanksgiving,
present your requests to God.
And the peace of God,
which transcends all understanding,
will guard your hearts and minds in Christ Jesus.
Philippians 4:6-7 NIV

If you need wisdom, ask our generous God,
and he will give it to you.
He will not rebuke you for asking.
James 1:5 NLT

Thomas and Janice's reluctance to assist left me with no familial support. Turning to Eli and Barry for solace, I implored them to pray for God's intervention. Eli's unexpected offer for Peter and me to relocate with him seemed like a beacon of hope, albeit complicated by legal constraints. Despite my trepidation, I felt compelled by the Holy Spirit to consider Eli's proposal. Summoning courage, I contacted the courthouse, navigating the intricate process of appealing to the court and Irvin for permission to move out-of-state, a journey fraught with uncertainty yet guided by faith.Bowing my head in prayer, I beseech God for courage and the gift of words to stir compassion and empathy within both the judge and Irvin.

Have I not commanded thee?
Be strong and of good courage;
be not afraid, neither be thou dismayed;
for the LORD thy God is with thee
whithersoever thou goest.
Joshua 1:9 KJV

Then the LORD reached out his hand
and touched my mouth and said to me,
"I have put my words in your mouth."
Jeremiah 1:9 NIV

Armed with determination, I visited the local library, where I meticulously composed and printed three copies of my letter–one for myself, one for the judge, and one for Irvin. With a silent plea to the heavens, I entrusted the letters to the post office, sending them via certified mail. As anticipated, the inevitable challenge from Irvin arrived promptly after 21 days, heralding the arrival of a court notification for late October 2019. Throughout this turbulent period, I leaned heavily on the support of Eli and Barry, finding solace in prayer and camaraderie. Yet, amidst my struggles, I couldn't shake the unsettling feeling of being watched. Suspicious of my mother's behavior, I noticed her surreptitious eavesdropping on my conversations and private phone calls, leading me to speculate on potential collusion with Irvin or his family.

Peter's fifth birthday was approaching, and I decided on a quaint celebration at the nearby park in town. Gathering the essentials, I procured three pizzas, adorned the space with decorations, and secured a cake fit for the occasion. With Peter's gifts neatly wrapped, I crafted a heartfelt invitation, extending it to Irvin, Stephanie, Greta, Thomas, Janice, and my nephews. On the day of the festivities, I chauffeured Peter and my mother to the park, pizzas in tow. We set up the decorations, and our guests began to trickle in. Irvin, accompanied by Stephanie and her grandson Alvin, arrived first, followed by Jerome, a friend of Irvin's. Though Thomas was occupied with work, Janice and my nephews, James and Norton, joined us. The gathering was rounded out by the arrival of Greta, along with her granddaughters Celeste and Paula. Yet, amidst the joyous occasion, an uneasy atmosphere pervaded, as I noticed my mother engaging in hushed conversations with Greta, Janice, and Stephanie.

Overwhelmed by the palpable tension and the unsettling air thick with whispers, I felt a sense of foreboding as I observed the covert exchanges between my mother and Irvin's mother. In the midst of the discomfort, I turned inward, entreating God for the fortitude to navigate the storm brewing around me.

So do not fear, for I am with you;
do not be dismayed, for I am your God.
I will strengthen you and help you;
I will uphold you with my righteous right hand.
Isaiah 41:10 NIV

As the festivities wound down and guests began to depart, Greta, Celeste, and Paula bid their farewells, leaving me to tackle the aftermath of the celebration. Amidst the cleanup, Irvin approached me with a request to take Peter for the weekend. Despite my reservations, I acquiesced, gathering Peter's gifts and facilitating the transfer. Strangely, my mother took charge of distributing the remaining pizza to Janice, a gesture that left me feeling aggravated. As Irvin and Stephanie prepared to depart with Peter, they requested the use of my car seat, promising to return it promptly. Standing by, I obliged, but what followed was a shocking barrage of insults and threats from both Irvin and Stephanie, delivered in the presence of innocent bystanders. Their vitriolic tirade, laced with profanities, was an attempt to undermine my confidence as a mother and cast doubt on my hopes for a better future.

O generation of vipers,
how can ye,
being evil, speak good things?
For out of the abundance of the heart
the mouth speaketh.
Matthew 12:34 KJV

Feeling utterly betrayed and wounded by the venomous words hurled at me, not just by Irvin and Stephanie, but also by my own mother and Janice, I found myself at a loss for words. Summoning what little strength remained within me, I mustered a simple declaration, refusing to subject myself to further abuse. Ignoring Janice's feeble attempt to salvage the situation with hollow professions of love, I retreated to my car, leaving behind the toxic atmosphere. With a heavy heart and simmering anger, I drove home in silence, each passing mile a painful reminder of the betrayal I had endured from those closest to me.

> *"For even your brothers and the house of your father,*
> *even they have dealt treacherously with you;*
> *they are in full cry after you;*
> *do not believe them,*
> *though they speak friendly words to you."*
> **Jeremiah 12:6 ESV**

In the sanctuary of my bedroom, I allowed the floodgates of emotion to burst forth, tears streaming down my cheeks as I poured out my heart to God. Despite the overwhelming pain and betrayal, I found comfort in the belief that He was with me, a steadfast presence amidst the turmoil. In the depths of my despair, I clung to the assurance of His unfailing love, finding strength in the threefold cord within me.

> *The LORD is close to the brokenhearted;*
> *he rescues those whose spirits are crushed.*
> **Psalm 34:18 NLT**

Amidst the torrent of tears and overwhelming emotions, I sensed the gentle embrace of the Holy Spirit, offering solace and reassurance in the midst of my anguish. Despite the tumultuous circumstances, I clung to the unwavering belief that, ultimately, everything would be alright. However, the weight of living under the same roof with someone whose intentions were anything but pure weighed heavily on my spirit. As I braced myself to face another day, a gnawing sense of foreboding gnawed at the pit of my stomach. With the court date looming just two days away, and still reeling from the fallout of Peter's birthday party, I couldn't shake the feeling that darker times lay ahead.

Irvin sent a text requesting an overnight stay with Peter. I agreed, yet insisted we meet in a public place. The exchange with Stephanie was at a grocery store 2 towns away, and had left me with a lingering sense of unease, a foreboding feeling that refused to be silenced. As I drove home from the meeting place, my heart heavy with worry, I turned to prayer, pleading for guidance and strength to face the uncertainty ahead. Trusting in the Lord's wisdom, I sought to relinquish my fear and place my faith in His plan.

The next day, I arrived at the designated meeting spot, only to find it eerily deserted. Panic rose within me as I realized something was terribly wrong. With trembling hands, I reached out to Eli, seeking solace and counsel in his steadfast presence. His advice to involve the authorities resonated with me, and I called the police in both cities involved. However, their response, citing legal constraints, only added to my despair. In a state of utter distress, I leaned on Eli for support as I made the agonizing journey back to my mother's house, emotionally preparing myself for the looming court date. Despite the turmoil and uncertainty, I clung to the hope that justice would prevail, trusting in God's unfailing grace to see me through the darkness.

As I stood outside the courtroom, clutching my Bible tightly, I drew strength from the prayers of Eli and Barry, their support and a comforting presence amidst my anxiety and fear. With each passing moment, I reaffirmed my faith that God was by my side, guiding me through the tumultuous journey ahead.

The arrival of Irvin, Stephanie, Greta, and Irvin's grandmother Janet only served to intensify the tension in the air, their disdainful glares a stark reminder of the adversarial nature of the situation. I stepped into the courtroom. The judge offered a daunting suggestion: Irvin could keep Peter and I could relocate to Arizona. Though his words offered a potential solution, it filled me with apprehension and uncertainty. The thought of entrusting Peter's well-being to individuals struggling with substance abuse and mental instability was a terrifying prospect, challenging me to reconcile my desires with the harsh realities of the situation. Yet, even in the face of adversity, I remained steadfast in my faith, trusting that God's plan would ultimately guide me towards the path of righteousness and protection for both Peter and me.

In the aftermath of the courthouse ordeal, the weight of the situation bore me down, leaving me overwhelmed with conflicting emotions. As I rode the elevator with Irvin, Stephanie, Greta, and Janet, a palpable tension hung in the air, each moment fraught with discomfort and uncertainty.

Retreating to the solitude of my car, I found myself besieged by a barrage of calls and messages from Irvin and Greta, pleading for a meeting outside the courthouse. Sensing the urgency in their demands, I made a conscious decision to prioritize my own well-being and safety, ignoring their pleas and seeking refuge in the counsel of Eli. With Eli's prayers offering a beacon of hope amidst the chaos, I grappled with the daunting choice before me–to remain in a toxic environment or to break free in search of healing and restoration. Encouraged by Eli's words and reminded of the abuse I had endured, I resolved to leave, gathering my belongings and preparing to embark on a journey toward a brighter future.

As I faced the inevitable confrontation with my mother, I remained steadfast in my resolve, asserting my decision with calm determination. Despite her protests and accusations, I stood firm, trusting in God's guidance and refusing to be swayed by her manipulative tactics. With a heavy heart and a solemn sense of purpose, I bid farewell to my mother and the tumultuous environment that had plagued me for so long. I set out on a path towards healing and redemption, guided by faith and fortified by the support of those who believed in me.

Embarking on the journey to my new destination, a mix of trepidation and determination coursed through my veins. With only three months of driving experience under my belt, each mile was a testament to my courage and resilience. Guided by the steady voice of my GPS and the comforting presence of God, I kept the music off, allowing the silence to be filled with whispered prayers and heartfelt conversations. Each stop along the way, whether for gas, food, or rest, offered a brief respite from the road, a chance to rejuvenate both body and spirit before pressing onward.

Despite the length of the journey, a sense of peace enveloped me, as if the Holy Spirit itself was guiding my every move. With each passing mile, I felt a renewed sense of strength and purpose, knowing that I was embarking on a path of healing and redemption, guided by faith, and fortified by God's presence that surrounded me.

For those who are led by the Spirit of God
are the children of God.
Romans 8:14 NIV

Arriving in Arizona, weary from the long journey, I pulled into a rest stop and sought solace in a brief nap, the soft hum of the surroundings lulling me into a much-needed reprieve. Awaking refreshed and rejuvenated, I resumed my drive, the anticipation of my final destination driving me forward. Upon arriving at Eli and Edward's house, a wave of relief washed over me, accompanied by a profound sense of gratitude for their unwavering support. With a renewed sense of purpose, I set about unloading my belongings, shedding the weight of the past and embracing the promise of a new beginning.

Deleting the messages and voicemails from Irvin, Greta, and Stephanie, I made a conscious choice to leave behind the negativity and turmoil that had plagued me, focusing instead on the blessings that awaited me in this new chapter of my life. As I settled into my temporary sanctuary, I allowed myself to finally rest, confident in the knowledge that I was exactly where I needed to be, surrounded by love, support, and the promise of a brighter tomorrow.

Navigating the unfamiliar terrain of being far from Peter weighed heavily on my heart, casting a shadow of sadness and longing over my days. Despite the challenges, Edward's warmth and kindness provided a beacon of light amidst the darkness, his companionship offering solace and comfort during Eli's absence at work.

Eli had suggested I assist Edward with his homeschooling, and I found a sense of purpose and fulfillment in contributing to his education. Creating a structured class schedule and organizing materials, I sought to support him in his studies, grateful for the chance to make a positive impact in his life. Eli's welcoming demeanor and his mother Harriet's kindness served as pillars of support during this trying time, their generosity and hospitality easing the burden of loneliness and isolation. Harriet's reassurance that I was always welcome in her home and her offer of assistance underscored the sense of belonging and community that I found in their midst, reminding me that I was not alone in this journey.

In the warmth of that devout family's embrace, I discovered an unexpected blessing: a profound sense of love and kindness enveloping me. As Eli and I tended to Edward, I found not just solace but also strength in our shared faith. Eli's unwavering support encouraged me to trust in my abilities and to boldly align myself with the values of Christ.

> *A final word:*
> *be strong in the LORD*
> *and in His Mighty power.*
> ***Ephesians 6:10 NLT***

During a particularly challenging phone call, I confronted my mother's hurtful words head-on, asserting my boundaries and refusing to tolerate further abuse. I hung up, a decision that marked a pivotal moment of empowerment for me. Despite my distance from Peter, I reached out to him over the phone, only to hear Irvin and Stephanie's attempts to poison his mind against me, urging him to express false hatred. While this intensified the struggle of being apart from Peter, it also served as a catalyst, fortifying my resolve to return home and engage in the legal battle for his custody.

> *"For they will fight you, but they will fail.*
> *For I am with you, and I will take care of you.*
> *I, the LORD, have spoken!"*
> ***Jeremiah 1:19 NLT***

After just two months of residing in Arizona with Eli and Edward, I mustered my courage and the $250 Barry had kindly provided for gas to make the journey back home. Knowing it would be arduous, I prepared myself as best I could for the long drive ahead. With no immediate place to stay upon my return, I resolved to explore options at women's shelters upon arrival. After a grueling 15-hour drive without rest, I finally parked in the lot of a department store. Caught off guard by the winter chill and ill-prepared for outdoor sleeping, I reached out to my chiropractor, Gloria, the only person I believed might lend a helping hand. I left a voicemail and was amazed when she promptly returned my call within 15 minutes, offering me refuge at her home and providing essential supplies —a sleeping bag, pillow, and blanket. Overwhelmed with gratitude, I accepted her aid, and before departing, Gloria shared information about a local organization offering women's shelter services, one I had yet to hear of. With this newfound knowledge, I resolved to explore this option the following week.

Although my mother had been dismissive, I reached out to her again upon arriving in town, hoping for a temporary place to stay. However, her abrupt refusal and unkind tone left me without shelter for the weekend. Fortunately, Gloria came to my rescue once again, offering the parking lot of her chiropractic clinic as a safe spot for me to rest. Grateful for her kindness, I spent two frigid nights sleeping in my car, the temperature dropping to a chilly 38 degrees. It was the sleeping bag, pillow, and blanket provided by Gloria that kept me warm and shielded from the biting cold. As I sought solace in the words of my Bible, illuminated by the faint glow of my cell phone, I remained hidden under the blanket, wary of drawing attention to my unconventional sleeping arrangements. A police car patrolled the parking lot during the night, but the officer never approached my vehicle, allowing me to rest undisturbed.

> *A thousand may fall at your side*
> *and ten thousand at your right hand,*
> *but danger will not come near you.*
> **Psalm 91:7 AMP**

On Sunday, my last night before my scheduled homelessness intake appointment, I found myself with only $10 to spare. Determined to refresh myself after three days without a shower, I headed to the local swimming pool and paid for access to their facilities. The sensation of warm water washing away the grime was a welcome relief.

After my shower, I made my way to the organization where I had initially planned to seek assistance. Yolanda, the woman I spoke with, conducted the intake process with compassion, asking each question with genuine concern. She assured me that she would personally reach out when my name came up on the shelter waiting list, offering a glimmer of hope. The following day, emboldened by Yolanda's kindness and determined to explore all options, I ventured to the organization recommended by Gloria, which offered a women's transitional living program.

During my intake interview with Olga, she gathered personal details to establish my client file. When I disclosed my homeless status, she swiftly inquired if I would be open to an interview for the local women's shelter, which operated as a transitional living program. Eager for any opportunity for stability, I expressed my interest, and within 15 minutes, I found myself in an interview with Violet, the program director. Violet's attentive demeanor and genuine concern resonated deeply with me as I shared my story. What truly moved me was her offer to pray for me. In that moment, her heartfelt prayer, perfectly attuned to my needs, enveloped me in a sense of comfort and reassurance.

> *A word fitly spoken is like apples of gold*
> *in pictures of silver.*
> **Proverbs 25:11 KJV**

Violet's swift action left me stunned and grateful. Within just an hour of our interview, she called to inform me that a bed was available at the shelter, instructing me to arrive within the next hour. Witnessing the rapid response, I marveled at how God's intervention seemed to be at work through Violet and the shelter staff, orchestrating my path to stability.

Despite my gratitude, nervous anticipation gnawed at me as I contemplated what awaited me at the shelter. The prospect of spending my first night in unfamiliar surroundings filled me with apprehension. Nevertheless, I resolved to face this new experience head-on. Arriving precisely at the time and location Violet had provided, I took a deep breath and stepped forward, ready to embrace whatever lay ahead.

Upon my arrival at the shelter, I was greeted by a kind-hearted woman named Sandra, who warmly welcomed me and guided me through the initial steps. She graciously offered to assist with my belongings, explaining that they would be washed and sanitized for cleanliness as a precaution against bed bugs. Sandra also recommended laundering the clothes I was currently wearing before entering the shelter. Taking note of my needs, Sandra swiftly provided me with fresh clothes to change into after my shower. Her thoughtful gesture eased my transition into this new environment. After I freshened, Sandra extended her kindness further by offering to purchase lunch from Subway, ensuring that I felt nourished and cared for during this pivotal moment of transition.

Sandra's thoughtful guidance continued as she led me upstairs for a tour of the shelter, where I discovered two other women already in residence. As we walked through the space, Sandra pointed out the eight beds available, some of which were bunk beds, and kindly informed me that I could select whichever bed suited me best. Opting for a single bed tucked away in the corner, I felt a sense of comfort and privacy in my chosen spot.

Sandra then provided me with fresh sheets, blankets, and a pillow and pillowcase, inviting me to make my bed and arrange my belongings to my liking. She showed me my designated space in the closet, ensuring I had room to store my belongings, and pointed out a Rubbermaid tote beneath the bed for additional clothing storage. With Sandra's guidance and the welcoming atmosphere of the shelter, I began to settle into my new surroundings, grateful for the sense of security and belonging that awaited me.

Wanting to travel lightly, I packed my clothes into a backpack and my toiletries into a shopping bag. Initially, sharing living quarters with unfamiliar women felt somewhat awkward. However, I soon discovered that while we were still acquaintances, the other residents were courteous and welcoming. Each of us had assigned chores and tasks to complete weekly, which fostered a sense of shared responsibility and community within the shelter.

I obtained permission from the resident manager to attend a Wednesday evening church dinner and Bible study with Rachel, a friend I had met while working at the thrift store a year prior. During my first dinner there, as I disposed of my paper plate, I struck up a conversation with a friendly woman about my experiences at the shelter. To my surprise, another woman overheard our discussion and revealed herself as my assigned mentor for the shelter. Her name was Abigail.

Abigail's presence was a welcome addition to my experience at the shelter. We initially met during a scheduled class, but our connection extended beyond those sessions as we began meeting outside of the structured environment. Her kindness, encouragement, and attentive ear became invaluable sources of support during some of my most challenging moments. Through our interactions, I found solace and strength, knowing that I had someone like Abigail by my side.

Following the Bible study, a woman approached me with a warm smile and introduced herself as Cherish. She explained that a sense of divine prompting had led her to initiate a conversation with me. Cherish asked if we could exchange numbers, a gesture that I welcomed wholeheartedly. With a shared connection formed through our faith and interaction, we exchanged contact information, paving the way for what I hoped would be a meaningful connection and source of support in the days to come.

Understand (this), my beloved brethren.
Let every man be quick to hear (a ready listener),
slow to speak, slow to take offense and to get angry.
James 1:19 AMPC

He who is gracious and lends a hand to the poor
lends to the LORD,
and the LORD will repay him for his good deed.
Proverbs 19:17 AMP

Amidst the demands of my online college education, I diligently pursued job opportunities to support myself. After applying to a restaurant, I received a prompt callback and progressed swiftly through the interview and hiring process. Eager to reconnect with Peter, I called Irvin's phone to arrange a meeting, hoping to spend quality time with my son over lunch. However, my efforts were thwarted when Irvin and Stephanie intercepted the call, preventing me from speaking directly to Peter. Despite my earnest request to arrange a visit, they remained unyielding, denying me the chance to reconnect with my son.

Irvin and Stephanie continued to block my attempts to see Peter with various excuses, but I persisted. When they wouldn't provide a time when

Peter was available, Stephanie took over the conversation, resorting to verbal abuse and profanity. Faced with such hostility, I ended the call and acted the following day by filing legal paperwork at the courthouse with Rachel's help.

A court date was set for a few weeks later. On that day, I took the day off from work and was accompanied by my friend Rachel and Delilah, the live-in resident manager at the shelter. Delilah offered a heartfelt prayer for strength and guidance before we entered the courthouse. Moments later, Thomas, accompanied by Irvin, entered the courtroom, further escalating the tension surrounding Thomas' presence and the legal proceedings.

In the courtroom, the judge addressed Irvin's claims regarding my lack of attempted contact with Peter, which I refuted, providing the true account of our interactions. Recognizing the importance of a mother's relationship with her child, the judge ruled that Irvin could not withhold Peter from me.

Turning to me, the judge inquired about my living situation and employment status. Despite being in a women's shelter, I explained my progress towards stability, including my job and imminent housing prospects. Acknowledging my efforts, the judge granted me two weekly visits with Peter: one hour-long visit on Wednesdays and a two-hour visit every Saturday. Furthermore, the judge ordered mediation between Irvin and me to address ongoing custody issues, with the expectation of transitioning to overnight visits once I secured stable housing. This decision filled me with gratitude and reassurance; I felt as though divine favor was guiding my path forward.

May the favor of the LORD our God rest on us;
establish the work of our hands for us—
yes, establish the work of our hands.
Psalm 90:17 NIV

Violet, the program director, had recommended a therapist named Isabella, and I promptly contacted Isabella and scheduled a session with her. We met the day after the court hearing, and the meeting marked the beginning of a significant chapter in my healing journey. Unlike previous therapists, Isabella immediately fostered a sense of safety and trust during our initial session. She took the time to genuinely get to know me without pressuring me to delve into serious topics prematurely. Despite the gentle nature of our conversation, I felt comfortable enough to open up about the distressing experience of Peter being taken by Irvin and Stephanie. Sharing this painful event with Isabella felt like a small but crucial step toward healing, laying the foundation for future progress and growth. With Isabella's guidance and support, I embarked on a journey of healing and self-discovery, knowing that I was in capable hands.

Rachel's unwavering support during the visits with Peter was invaluable. She provided emotional support and acted as a witness to any interactions with Irvin and Stephanie. Her presence brought me comfort and strength during those challenging times, and I was deeply grateful for her friendship.

I encouraged Rachel to pursue her education by obtaining her GED. She embraced the idea enthusiastically, so I took her to the local community college to enroll in classes. After leaving the college, we made a quick stop at the library to return some books I had borrowed. As we pulled out of the library parking lot, a speeding car careened around the corner, colliding with the driver's side rear tire of my car. The impact sent us spinning across two lanes of traffic, a terrifying experience that left us shaken and thankful to have escaped serious injury.

As I approached Rachel, uncertainty lingered in her eyes, mirroring my own feelings. Scanning the surroundings, I searched for the man responsible for the collision, hoping to settle matters swiftly. Yet, he was nowhere in sight. With anxiety, I maneuvered my car out of the traffic jam. As I turned back, my gaze caught the man in his vehicle. Determined, I strode towards him, intent on exchanging insurance details. The pungent scent of alcohol emanating from him raised immediate concern. "Why do you smell like alcohol?" I inquired, but he remained silent, offering his insurance card for me to capture with my phone.

Navigating through the bustling streets, I managed to safely escort Rachel and myself back home. However, the ordeal was far from over. In addition to juggling my college assignments, job responsibilities, and duties for the shelter program, I now found myself grappling with the aftermath of the car accident. Despite the mounting pressure, I made sure to keep Violet informed of the situation. To my relief, she offered unwavering support and understanding, even extending her prayers for my well-being.

The prayer of a righteous person
has great power as it is working.
James 5:16 ESV

When Rachel and I returned to the shelter,, a resident named Frieda approached me with a troubling revelation. She had stumbled upon a Facebook post shared by the wife of the man who collided with my car. To my dismay, the post falsely accused me of being responsible for the accident. It felt like a spiritual attack after what I perceived as a triumph of good over evil in the courthouse.

A false witness will not go unpunished,
and he who breathes out lies will perish.
Proverbs 19:9 NIV

If you set a trap for others,
you will get caught in it yourself.
If you roll a boulder down on others,
it will crush you instead.
Proverbs 26:27 NLT

About a month later, and just eight days after celebrating my birthday, Violet delivered incredible news—I had been approved for an apartment! It was an unexpected turn of events sparked by a conversation between Violet and Isabelle, the apartment manager. Isabelle had reached out to Violet seeking recommendations for potential tenants, and Violet had wasted no time in mentioning my name. I was already on the apartment waiting list. Isabelle promptly contacted me, eager to arrange my move-in date. With excitement coursing through me, I informed her that I could transition into the apartment within two days.

The day before my scheduled move into the apartment, I gathered Delilah and my roommates at the shelter to share the exciting news. Delilah, ever the compassionate soul, immediately sprang into action.

Utilizing her connections with the non-profit organization she was involved with, she arranged for movers to assist with the transition. Together, we coordinated the acquisition of essential furnishings: beds for both myself and Peter, two end tables, a lamp, a dining room table with four chairs, and a dresser for Peter. Delilah's generosity didn't stop there; she dipped into her own funds to purchase kitchen and toiletry supplies, leaving me overwhelmed with gratitude. The financial aspect was also taken care of seamlessly. The first organization I had an intake with covered the security deposit, while the non-profit organization Violet worked for generously covered the prorated amount of rent. Reflecting on the journey from my arrival at the shelter to the imminent move into my own apartment, I couldn't help but feel immense gratitude. In just two months and ten days, by the grace of God, I had transitioned from uncertainty to newfound stability. Glory be to God indeed!

For I assure you and most solemnly say to you,
if you have (living) faith the size of a mustard seed,
you will say to this mountain,
'Move from here to there,'
and (if it is God's Will) it will move;
and nothing will be impossible for you.
Matthew 17:20 AMP

Enter His gates with thanksgiving
and His courts with praise;
give thanks to Him and praise His Name.
Psalm 100:4 NIV

And my God will liberally supply
(fill until full) your every need
according to His riches in glory in Christ Jesus.
Philippians 4:19 AMP

Chapter Eight

A NEW CREATION

With rent looming and my bank account dwindling to less than $500, anxiety crept in. Recalling a conversation with my new friend Cherish from Bible study, I remembered her advice to seek assistance from the church elders. Nervously, I mustered the courage to pray for guidance before making the call. After dialing the number, I was greeted warmly by Robert's wife, Pearl. Our conversation flowed effortlessly–we discussed the church and my desire to attend Sunday services. When Robert joined the call, his attentive demeanor eased my nerves as I poured out my financial struggles. He promptly informed me that the church was willing to extend a helping hand and assured me that he would consult with the other elders. I was overwhelmed with gratitude, and tears of relief streamed down my cheeks. In that moment, I felt enveloped by God's kindness and provision, reassured that I was not alone in my journey.

In His kindness God called you
to share in His eternal glory by means of Christ Jesus.
So after you have suffered a little while,

he will restore, support, and strengthen you,
and he will place you on a firm foundation.
1 Peter 5:10 NLT

A few weeks later, Irvin and I had our first mediation session over the phone. As tensions flared and Irvin unleashed a torrent of objections, vehemently denying any rights for Peter's mother, I found an unexpected surge of boldness within me. With unwavering conviction, I addressed Irvin, calmly asserting the truth: "With all due respect, if you had not taken Peter against his will, this situation wouldn't have arisen." Irvin hurled profanities at me before abruptly disconnecting the call, leaving a palpable silence in its wake.The mediator Lucy's voice broke through the quiet as she attempted to reconnect with Irvin, only to be met with the hollow sound of a disconnected line. Despite the abrupt end to the mediation session, my resolve remained unwavering. Lucy dutifully relayed the events to the judge, and to my surprise, I received news shortly after a visitation schedule had been arranged, granting me the opportunity to pick up Peter for his first overnight visit the following day. It was a pivotal moment, marking a step forward in reclaiming a sense of normalcy amid the turmoil.

The court ordered Irvin to provide his residential address so I could pick Peter up—and the location turned out to be Stephanie's brother's house. For added support and security, Abigail accompanied me on the journey, prepared to act as a witness in case tensions escalated between Irvin and Stephanie. Upon our arrival, Abigail and I were met with an unsettling sight: a disheveled couple, a man and woman seemingly under the influence of drugs, loitering outside the residence. Undeterred, I dialed Irvin's number, announcing my presence to collect Peter.

When Peter emerged, his eyes sparkled with excitement at the prospect of spending the night. His enthusiasm mirrored my own; the brief visits we'd shared weren't nearly enough. In that moment, it felt as though God was orchestrating events, paving the way for Peter's eventual return home with me. The anticipation of having him under my roof filled me with a profound sense of hope and gratitude.

Oh, how great is Your goodness
to those who publicly declare that You will rescue them.
For You have stored up great blessings
for those who trust and reverence You.
Psalm 31:19 TLB

Seeing Peter's delight as he discovered his own bedroom, adorned with posters and toys, I found my own joy amplified by his happiness. Witnessing his excitement was a balm to my soul, serving as a reminder of the newfound stability we were building together. Yet, amidst this moment of joy, a shadow loomed from my workplace. A threatening encounter with a customer had shaken me to the core, exacerbated by the management's indifference to my safety concerns. Recognizing the toll it took on my already burdened shoulders, I made the difficult decision to resign from my position at the restaurant. Summoning courage, I reached out to my shift supervisor, detailing the incident and explaining the overwhelming stress it added to my already tumultuous situation with Irvin in court. To my relief, she offered understanding and support, granting me the space I needed to navigate this period of transition.

In the days that followed, I turned to prayer, seeking solace and guidance from God. Alongside Violet's comforting presence, I immersed myself in deep contemplation, fervently seeking God's wisdom and direction for the next chapter of my life.

Call to me and I will answer you
and tell you great and unsearchable things
you do not know.
Jeremiah 33:3 NIV

On the seventh day following my departure from the restaurant, a glimmer of hope emerged in the form of an opening at the non-profit organization where Violet was employed. Eager to explore this opportunity, I promptly forwarded my resume to Laura, the executive director, expressing my interest in contributing to their cause.

To my surprise and delight, Laura reached out to me the very next day to discuss the potential of joining their team. While the position they were offering required a level of commitment I wasn't quite prepared for, I didn't hesitate to convey my willingness to utilize my spiritual gifts to benefit others within the organization. After thoughtful consideration, Laura extended an offer for me to join as an office assistant to the volunteers. It was a role that resonated with me, allowing me to play a part in supporting the organization's mission while easing into the transition from my previous job. With gratitude and anticipation, I embraced this new opportunity, ready to embark on a journey of service and purpose.

Embracing the new opportunity bestowed upon me, I wasted no time in extending my gratitude to the restaurant's shift supervisor while tendering my resignation. The decision to depart from my former workplace was anchored in the belief that this new role aligned better with my circumstances and aspirations. With Peter's welfare at the forefront of my mind, I immediately communicated with Laura, my new employer, regarding my current custody battles and court proceedings. Transparency was essential to me, as I wanted to ensure that Peter remained my top priority. Laura exhibited understanding and empathy, assuring me that she fully comprehended the significance of Peter's well-being in my life. Her unwavering support and understanding reaffirmed my belief that I had made the right decision in joining the non-profit organization. With a newfound sense of reassurance, I embarked on this new chapter with the confidence that my priorities were understood and respected.

As an office assistant to the volunteers at the non-profit organization, I found fulfillment in every task, big or small. Conducting telephone intake interviews with incoming clients provided me with a profound opportunity to connect with individuals, to listen to their stories, and to offer words of encouragement and prayer. Each conversation was a reminder of the resilience of the human spirit and the power of compassion in fostering hope. Guiding individuals through their journey with empathy and understanding, I felt privileged to walk alongside them, even if only for a brief moment in their lives.

Creating files for these individuals, organizing their information with care and attention to detail, felt like more than just administrative work— it was a tangible way of extending a helping hand, of ensuring that their needs were met with dignity and respect. Every interaction reaffirmed my belief that I was exactly where I was meant to be, blessed with the opportunity to give back to the place that had once lifted me up in my time of need. In serving others, I found a sense of purpose and fulfillment that transcended the confines of a job title—it was a calling, a way of expressing gratitude for the blessings I had received.

From the fruit of their lips
people are filled with good things,
and the work of their hands brings them reward.
Proverbs 12:14 NIV

During my tenure at the non-profit organization, my commitment to Peter did not waver. Despite the demands of my job, I kept up regular overnight visits with Peter, particularly during the summertime when our bond could flourish without the constraints of school schedules. As I balanced work and parenting responsibilities, Abigail emerged as a beacon of support and generosity. Recognizing the challenges I faced, she selflessly offered to care for Peter while I worked, alleviating the burden of childcare and allowing me to focus on my professional duties. What's more, her kindness extended beyond mere assistance—Abigail refused to accept any form of payment for her services, embodying a true spirit of friendship and compassion.

He who is gracious and lends a hand to the poor
lends to the LORD,
and the LORD will repay him for his good deed.
Proverbs 19:17 AMP

One day, suddenly amidst the whirlwind of my duties at the non-profit organization, Irvin's persistent calls pierced through the bustling atmosphere and stirred apprehension within me. When I confided in Violet, she pointed out that it must be urgent and persuaded me to find out what was going on. Stepping into the hallway to return Irvin's call, I braced myself for the news that awaited. His voice trembled with urgency as he relayed the grave threat posed by the encroaching wildfires, compelling them to evacuate immediately. In that moment, the gravity of the situation sank in, and I knew I needed to ensure Peter's safety at all costs.

As Irvin's words echoed in my mind, clarity descended upon me like a guiding light. This was no mere coincidence but God's intervention, orchestrating Peter's return to my care. I confided in Laura, the executive director, explaining the circumstances and my decision to depart from my role to prioritize Peter's well-being and facilitate his seamless transition into school. Though my tenure at the non-profit organization was brief, its impact was profound. Filled with purpose and meaning, it had prepared me for the challenges that lay ahead as I embarked on this new chapter as Peter's guardian once more.

As I left work and embarked on the 40-mile journey to Peter, Irvin, and Stephanie, the ominous veil of smoke shrouded the landscape, impairing visibility. I navigated cautiously through the thick haze, inching forward until I reached their location. Upon arrival, I texted Irvin, informing him of my presence. Moments later, Peter emerged, his face alight with joy at the prospect of returning home with me. However, I sensed Irvin's fear as he spoke of their uncertain future amidst the wild-fires. Despite knowing Irvin's aversion to faith, I felt compelled to offer a prayer for their safety and comfort. With Irvin's reluctant acceptance, I closed my eyes and lifted my voice in supplication, entreating God to bring solace and protection to Irvin, Stephanie, and her brother, guiding them to a place of safety amidst the chaos. In that fleeting moment of shared vulnerability, faith transcended barriers, uniting us in a collective plea for God's intervention. As I bid them farewell and drove away with Peter, I prayed fervently that God would heed our supplications.

But I say unto you,
love your enemies,
bless them that curse you,
do good to them that hate you,
and pray for them that despitefully use you,
and persecute you.
Matthew 5:44 KJV

After ensuring Peter's safety by bringing him home, the next crucial step was to enroll him in kindergarten. Irvin suggested that Peter attend an elementary school near him. I promptly contacted the teacher to arrange a meeting and procure the necessary materials for Peter's online kindergarten, given the ongoing pandemic restrictions. The meeting at the school drew near, and Irvin insisted on personally escorting Peter to his first day of school. However, Peter seemed reluctant to be separated from me. Sensing the unease, I proposed a compromise: that we all enter the school together, fostering a sense of unity and support for Peter during this transitional period. In that moment, amidst the uncertainty and apprehension, the importance of prioritizing Peter's emotional well-being became abundantly clear. As we walked through the school doors as a united front, I held onto the hope that this collective effort would lay the foundation for a successful and harmonious journey through kindergarten, setting the stage for Peter's academic and personal growth in the years to come.

Despite Irvin's verbal protests, he eventually acquiesced and accompanied both Peter and me into the school. As we met with the teacher and received the necessary materials for Peter's virtual learning, tensions simmered beneath the surface. After the meeting, Irvin approached me with a request to take Peter out to lunch. Despite my previous plans, I agreed, informing Irvin that I would return to pick up Peter in an hour and a half. I decided to use the time to visit a natural grocery store to pick up some items I needed, finding solace in the familiar pages of my Bible as I waited. When the time came, I retrieved Peter from Irvin and Stephanie's place without any complications or resistance, and I was grateful for the peaceful resolution amidst the strained circumstances.

The following week, I sat beside Peter as he embarked on his online kindergarten journey, guiding him to concentrate and remain attentive. Amidst this, I noticed additional tasks demanding my attention: scheduling a doctor's appointment for Peter to renew his ADHD medication and facilitating his enrollment in our local school district. With determination, I accomplished both, efficiently communicating with the previous school district to return the Chromebook and transfer Peter's enrollment. Ensuring Peter's education remained uninterrupted, I diligently reviewed the lessons taught by his teacher during his offline hours.

As the school year reached its midpoint for Peter, an email from Violet illuminated a potential job opportunity.Laura had forwarded the job opportunity to Violet—a directorial role at another non-profit organization dedicated to serving the underprivileged in our community. Though the compensation didn't promise financial abundance, the prospect of making a meaningful impact resonated deeply with me, aligning with my faith and sense of purpose in serving both the community and God's Kingdom. Despite anticipating the challenges ahead, I sensed a compelling call from the Holy Spirit to pursue this opportunity. I submitted my resume and promptly received an invitation for an interview. Violet graciously agreed to look after Peter while I interviewed. Stepping into the meeting room, I encountered Pastor Theodore, who oversaw the non-profit's endeavors, alongside the incumbent director, Ariel, and several other church elders and volunteers. To my surprise, a panel of eight individuals awaited, ready to delve into my qualifications and aspirations.

Despite the intimidating panel of eight interviewers, I remained composed, recognizing each individual's genuine interest in getting to know me through their thoughtful inquiries about my experiences. With honesty and vulnerability, I shared my journey of overcoming homelessness, highlighting the invaluable support I had received from various non-profit organizations in the community. As the interview progressed, I was pleasantly surprised when the questions shifted from qualifications to availability, prompting me to explain my role as a single parent to a special needs child. Emphasizing the importance of meeting Peter's needs, I proposed bringing him along due to my current commitment to home-schooling. I told the interview team I would coordinate with Peter's school, ensuring seamless continuation of his education while he accompanied me to work. The interview panel's remarkable understanding and accommodation affirmed that this job was indeed part of God's plan, tailored to fit both my professional aspirations and my responsibilities as a single parent.

Love never gives up,
never loses faith,

is always hopeful,
and endures through every circumstance.
1 Corinthians 13:7 NLT

Amidst the initial challenges of my new role, which involved establishing firm boundaries both at the center where we provided aid and in my personal life with Irvin and Stephanie, I felt the hand of God guiding me. After less than a month at my new job, Pastor Lucas, from my church, introduced me to Walter, a young man under his mentorship. Walter told me about Britney, a homeless young woman in desperate need. Witnessing her visibly distressed state, I approached her with compassion, assuring her of my willingness to assist once I understood her situation better. Britney courageously shared her harrowing experiences as a 20-year-old runaway survivor of multiple instances of sexual abuse. Recognizing the urgency of her need for shelter and support, I immediately reached out to a nearby youth center, securing an appointment for Britney. By the following day, Britney had found housing, a testament to the swift and tangible impact of God's grace and intervention. Praise be to God for His providence in this critical moment.

During this period, I grappled with intermittent discomfort from two front teeth that required root canal treatment. Approximately two years prior, dentists had diagnosed both teeth as cracked, prompting inquiries into my childhood activities. I had disclosed my history of abuse, which they empathetically acknowledged. However, around this time, both teeth began to loosen, necessitating a visit to the dentist. To my dismay, the prognosis revealed the inevitable extraction of both teeth, leaving me facing the prospect of dentures. The experience–particularly the loss of my front two teeth–was undeniably humiliating. Yet, in retrospect, it serves as a poignant reminder of the trials I've overcome and the blessings bestowed upon me by God's grace. Despite the initial shame, I'm now filled with gratitude for the ways in which God has delivered me from adversity.

As Peter entered first grade, the arrangement shifted to include overnight weekend visits with Irvin and Stephanie. Per the court order, Irvin was responsible for picking up Peter after school on Fridays, with me collecting him on Sunday afternoons. Recognizing the potential challenges posed by Irvin and Stephanie's behavior, I sought support from fellow church members and colleagues, including Sarah and Trudy, to accompany me during these pickups. Their presence served as a protective shield against any attempts by Irvin or Stephanie to manipulate the situation for their own ends. Through their unwavering support and solidarity, God provides strength and fortitude to navigate through these stressful and trying times. Their companionship became a tangible manifestation of divine grace, guiding me through the difficulties and challenges of co-parenting amidst adversity.

But the LORD stood at my side and gave me strength.
2 Timothy 4:17 NIV

One particular Sunday pickup, halfway through Peter's first-grade year, stands out vividly in my memory. Accompanied by Abigail, Peter and I arrived at the designated time, only to find Stephanie's mother, Kat's, vehicle parked in the driveway instead of Stephanie's. After I notified Irvin of our arrival, Kat emerged from the house and approached our vehicle. She told us that Irvin and Stephanie had raised concerns about Peter's well-being, prompting them to involve the Department of Human Services (DHS) and the police. Shocked and dismayed, I accepted a piece of paper containing contact information for a police officer. As Kat questioned whether I intended to contact Irvin again, I expressed gratitude for the information and bid her farewell before closing the door. In that moment of uncertainty and distress, the support and presence of Abigail and others served as a source of strength and reassurance, reminding me that we were not alone in facing these challenges.

Despite the unsettling situation, I found a sense of calm, fortified by the prayers and comforting presence of Abigail, who felt like family to me. Abigail urged me to reach out to the authorities for clarity. Gathering my resolve, I dialed the police, recounting the events and providing the information from the paper Kat had given me. The voice on the other end offered little insight, promising to investigate and call back. We waited expectantly in the neighborhood for nearly 20 minutes, but the anticipated call never came. Despite repeated attempts to reach the police, our efforts went unanswered.

Sensing the need to regroup and ease my mounting anxiety, Abigail offered prayers of comfort before driving me home. As the hours passed without any communication from the authorities, I made the decision to set aside my concerns for the remainder of the day, resolving to resume my efforts the following day. I sent Peter's teacher an email explaining the situation, informing her of Peter's absence until the legal matters were resolved and he could return to school safely.

The following day was consumed by urgent tasks as I diligently contacted Peter's mental health counselor and speech/occupational therapists, ensuring they were briefed on the distressing situation. With a heavy heart and determined resolve, I made my way to the courthouse to formally report the events that had transpired, seeking recourse through legal channels. In the midst of uncertainty and turmoil, I turned to prayer, seeking God's strength and guidance to navigate the challenges ahead. With a renewed sense of purpose, I searched for a lawyer, recognizing the importance of securing professional support to safeguard Peter's well-being and ensure justice prevailed. With each step, I leaned on my faith, trusting in God's providence to lead me through the darkness towards resolution and peace.

Look to the LORD and His strength;
seek His Face always.
Psalm 105:4 NIV

Amidst the initial setbacks in my search for legal representation, I found solace in prayer, trusting in God's guidance to lead me to the right lawyer. To my relief, an online search highlighted Timothy Allen, who boasted a reputation as one of the top family law lawyers in our state. I contacted his office and was met with kindness and efficiency as a receptionist promptly scheduled a consultation with Timothy. Two days later, I found myself speaking with Timothy, tasked with condensing the intricacies of my situation into a 30-minute conversation. With unwavering honesty, I laid bare the details of what had transpired, hoping to convey the urgency and gravity of the matter. Timothy's assurance that he would take on my case brought a sense of relief and hope. The retainer fee was $3,500, a significant portion of my savings. Yet, in that moment, the safety and well-being of Peter outweighed any financial concerns, reaffirming my unwavering commitment to securing his protection and justice, no matter the cost.

For we live by believing and not by seeing.
2 Corinthians 5:7 NLT

In a moment of both gratitude and uncertainty, I reached out to Pastor Lucas, Abigail's husband and the pastor of the church I had recently begun attending. I shared that I had found a lawyer and implored him to lift me up in prayer. Despite the looming financial strain, I knew deep down that pursuing legal action was imperative for Peter's safety. Summoning courage, I also approached Mark, the church treasurer, seeking assistance with the daunting legal costs. To my immense relief and gratitude, the church demonstrated unwavering support and solidarity, agreeing to cover the entire $3,500 retainer fee. It was a profound moment of affirmation, witnessing God's hand at work through the compassion and generosity of our church and community. United in prayer and purpose, we stood together to protect Peter and seek justice.

Therefore, as we have opportunity,
let us do good to all,
especially to those who are of the household of faith.
Galatians 6:10 NKJV

Confess your sins to each other
and pray for each other, so that you may be healed.
The earnest prayer of a righteous person
has great power
and produces wonderful results.
James 5:16 NLT

On the day of the court hearing, I found solace in the unwavering support of my church family, including Lucas, Abigail, Violet, Theodore, Drew, and Doris, whom I held in such high regard that I affectionately referred to them as Mom and Dad. Their presence at the courthouse served as a beacon of strength and solidarity. Timothy, our lawyer, was punctual and provided reassurance, explaining the legal proceedings and outlining the potential course of action should Irvin fail to comply with the court's directives. As Irvin arrived, Timothy accompanied me to approach the judge, ready to advocate for Peter's safe return home. With poise and determination, Timothy presented our case before the judge, who wasted no time in addressing Irvin directly, questioning his actions and urging him to account for his refusal to return Peter.

Next, Irvin presented his allegations, including disturbing claims of physical abuse and inappropriate behavior witnessed by members of the church. Sensing the urgency of the matter, the judge swiftly addressed Irvin's actions, probing into whether he had taken the necessary steps to report the alleged abuse to the appropriate authorities. Irvin's admission that he had contacted the Department of Human Services (DHS) but not Helping House prompted the judge to assert the need for a thorough investigation into the accusations.He emphasized that while an investigation would ensue, the immediate priority was to ensure Peter's safety and return him to my care. With firm resolve, the judge presented Irvin with two options: to arrange a time for Peter's return to my custody or to face the intervention of law enforcement to facilitate his safe retrieval.

Irvin's decision to allow me to pick up Peter from their residence later that day was met with a mixture of relief and apprehension. With the support and companionship of Lucas and Abigail, I went to Irvin and Stephanie's place to retrieve Peter. Following Peter's safe return, Lucas and Abigail extended an invitation to share a meal together, offering a moment of respite and connection amidst the turmoil.

He who is generous will be blessed,
for he gives some of his food to the poor.
Proverbs 22:9 AMP

But thanks be to God,
who gives us the victory (as conquerors)
through our Lord Jesus Christ.
1 Corinthians 15:57 AMP

Chapter Nine

OVERCOMER

And they overcame him by the blood of the Lamb,
and the word of their testimony.
Revelation 12:11 KJV

As I attended to the daily tasks of running the household and supporting Peter's return to normalcy, a knock on the door interrupted the routine. Welcoming the representatives from the Department of Human Services (DHS) into our home, I braced myself for a challenging conversation. They outlined the accusations made by Irvin during their visit to his and Stephanie's residence, and I recounted the events of the previous day with clarity and resolve. With Peter nearby, blissfully engaged in play, I offered reassurance of the loving and supportive environment he now had. Despite the trauma that lingered from the ordeal, I could see Peter's sense of contentment and security within the familiar surroundings of our home. In the face of adversity, my resolve remained unwavering, anchored by the love and stability that we sought to provide for Peter's well-being.

In the wake of the DHS visit, I found myself grappling with a myriad of emotions and concerns regarding Peter's well-being. As the workers shared their observations from their encounter with Irvin and Stephanie, including Greta's conspicuous presence, I felt a sense of unease deepening within me. Their suspicions only added to the gravity of the situation, reinforcing the urgency of seeking additional support for Peter's emotional recovery. Recalling the judge's recommendation to seek assistance from Helping House, I made a concerted effort to follow through, reaching out to schedule an appointment for Peter's assessment.

Recognizing the logistical challenges posed by Helping House's policy restricting parents from accompanying their children during appointments, I turned to Sarah, a dependable volunteer from my workplace who had consistently extended her support during weekend pickups from Irvin and Stephanie's place. I asked for her assistance in escorting Peter to his appointment, knowing that her compassionate presence would provide him with comfort and reassurance during this vulnerable time. Sarah's willingness to step in and offer her help reaffirmed God's providence in navigating through life's most trying moments. Together, we forged ahead, determined to ensure Peter received the care and support he needed to heal from the trauma he had endured.

Peter had been attending mental health counseling sessions, and at one of these sessions, Tracie, Peter's counselor, acted strangely. This unsettling encounter left me with a lingering sense of unease and suspicion. Her uncharacteristic behavior raised red flags in my mind. Upon confronting Tracie about her not inviting me back for the second half of Peter's session, her dismissive response only fueled my growing sense of distrust.

Determined to uncover the truth behind Tracie's sudden shift in demeanor and driven by a need to protect Peter, I resolved to uncover the truth. Through diligent probing, I unearthed unsettling revelations that Tracy had engaged in secret communications with Irvin, divulging the damning accusations he had levied against me to the judge and DHS. The puzzle pieces fell into place, elucidating the sinister forces at play behind Tracy's inexplicable behavior. It became abundantly clear that the sanctity of Peter's therapy sessions had been compromised, manipulated by external influences intent on tarnishing my character and undermining my efforts to safeguard Peter's well-being.

Navigating the complex legal terrain surrounding Peter's custody battle brought with it a new set of challenges and revelations. Irvin requested the notes from Peter's counseling sessions, and I immediately sought counsel from Timothy, my trusted legal advisor. Together, we devised a strategy to safeguard Peter's privacy and well-being while addressing the looming threat posed by Irvin's demands. In a proactive measure, I visited the counseling office to sign consent forms for both Irvin's and my own requests for Peter's counseling records. This preemptive step ensured that I maintained control over the dissemination of sensitive information, shielding Peter from potential exploitation. Timothy and I discussed the pressing issue of Irvin and Stephanie's continued drug use Timothy suggested petitioning the judge to order a hair follicle test for Irvin, a measure aimed at uncovering any substance abuse that could pose a threat to Peter's safety.

To my relief, the judge granted the request, issuing an order for Irvin to undergo the hair follicle test within a specified timeframe. This decisive action underscored the court's commitment to prioritizing Peter's well-being above all else. Amidst these legal maneuvers, Timothy confided in me about his own concerns for his daughter, revealing the profound impact of our shared experiences on those closest to us. As we navigated through the complex legal process, our bond strengthened, united by a shared commitment to protecting our loved ones and seeking justice in the face of adversity.

The deadline for Irvin's hair follicle test came and went, and he didn't take the test. Meanwhile, Timothy's diligent investigation unearthed troubling revelations about Irvin's substance abuse. Armed with this damning evidence, we returned to court, prepared to confront the stark reality of Irvin's actions. Despite Irvin's vehement denials, the judge's inquiry uncovered irrefutable proof of his drug use. The positive hair follicle test results for marijuana, methamphetamine, cocaine, and opiates painted a stark portrait of Irvin's disregard for the well-being of both himself, and those around him.

In light of this new information, the judge called for another hearing, setting the stage for a pivotal moment in Peter's custody battle. However, the hearing was postponed due to a scheduling error, leaving us all with a sense of frustration and uncertainty. Amidst the chaos and disappointment, I felt sought solace in the comforting embrace of prayer. Gathering with Timothy and our steadfast supporters from the church, we lifted our voices in collective supplication, beseeching God for divine intervention in both Timothy's personal struggles and the ongoing legal proceedings. In a moment of unity and faith, we entrusted our hopes and fears to God, seeking strength and guidance as we continued to navigate the turbulent waters of Peter's custody case.

Also, I tell you this:
If two of you agree here on earth
concerning anything you ask,
my Father in heaven will do it for you.
For where two or three gather together as my followers,
I am there among them.
Matthew 18:19-20 NLT

The anticipation leading up to the next court date felt like an eternity, punctuated by the relentless barrage of phone harassment from Irvin and Stephanie and the emotional toll of Peter's distressing weekend visits with them. Each visit left Peter emotionally shaken, adding another layer of complexity to an already challenging situation. I found myself contending not only with the relentless pressure from Irvin and Stephanie but also with the taxing dynamics of some of my colleagues at work. The cumulative weight of these challenges bore down heavily on me, threatening to overwhelm my resilience and resolve. Despite the overwhelming nature of these circumstances, I remained steadfast in my commitment to Peter's well-being, drawing strength from the unwavering support of my community and the unshakeable faith that guided me through the darkest of times. With each passing day, I clung to the hope that justice would prevail, determined to weather the storm and emerge stronger on the other side.

Amidst the emotional turmoil of Peter's custody battle and the relentless challenges I faced, I found solace in the unwavering support of my therapist, Isabella, whose guidance provided a lifeline during moments of uncertainty and despair. Additionally, the steadfast presence of Violet, Abigail, Lucas, and a host of cherished friends and members of my church family, including Drew, Doris, Douglas, Cherish, Paul, Nadine, Caroline, Travis, and Cheryl, served as a constant source of love, support, and encouragement.

And I will give you shepherds after my own heart,
who will guide you with knowledge and understanding.
Jeremiah 3:15 NLT

I sought the LORD and cried out to him in my afflictions,
and he helped me through all of the pain in the waiting.
In my distress I cried to the LORD, and He heard me.
Psalm 120:1 NKJV

The long-awaited court date arrived, but Irvin didn't show up. The judge facilitated Irvin's remote participation through a conference call. Timothy presented the damning evidence of Irvin's failed hair follicle test, advocating for sanctions to be imposed by the court. However, Irvin's response was one of defiance—he abruptly hung up rather than face the consequences of his actions. Undeterred by Irvin's evasion, the judge swiftly rendered a ruling, granting the motion for sanctions in light of the compelling evidence presented.

With the wheels of justice set in motion, the next court hearing was scheduled for a week and a half later, marking another crucial juncture in Peter's custody battle. Despite the challenges and setbacks encountered along the way, the pursuit of truth and justice remained steadfast, fueled by a determination to safeguard Peter's well-being at all costs.

Before the next hearing, however, Timothy urgently summoned me for a telephone hearing with the judge. With little time to spare, I hastily cleared my schedule, preparing myself for the weighty discussion that lay ahead. As the hearing commenced, Timothy and I found ourselves in disparate locations, connected only by the thread of telecommunication. Seeking privacy, I retreated to the sanctuary of my bedroom, the closed door offering a semblance of seclusion in the midst of the tumult. When questioned by the judge about my stance on custody arrangements, I spoke from the depths of my heart, articulating my fundamental concern for Peter's safety in light of Irvin's substance abuse. I asserted that sole custody was in Peter's best interest.

In a moment of clarity and resolution, the judge concurred, recognizing the paramount importance of safeguarding Peter's well-being. With a solemn decree, the judge granted me sole custody while also stipulating supervised visits for Irvin, ensuring a cautious approach to his involvement in Peter's life. With the weight of responsibility now squarely upon my shoulders, I embraced the newfound role of sole custodian with a sense of determination to provide Peter with the love, care, and security he deserved. Though the journey had been fraught with challenges and uncertainties, this moment marked a significant step forward in our quest for stability and peace.

But the LORD says,
"The captives of warriors will be released,
and the plunder of tyrants will be retrieved.
For I will fight those who fight you,
and I will save your children."
Isaiah 49:25 NLT

Chapter Ten
WITH GOD ALL THINGS ARE POSSIBLE

I n the nascent stages of this new legal arrangement, Irvin and Stephanie honored one scheduled visit, meeting us at a quaint restaurant in town. Among those present were Lucas, Abigail, and their sweet daughter Dawn, who came to provide unwavering support for Peter and me, doubling as vigilant guardians to prevent any attempt by Irvin or Stephanie to spirit Peter away. Soon after, Russell, a dedicated volunteer from my workplace, arrived to stand by Peter and me. My senses heightened, I remained vigilant, reassured by the presence of these allies who stood steadfastly at my side, ready to protect and support me through the ordeal.

> *But the LORD is faithful,*
> *and He will strengthen you*
> *(setting you on a firm foundation)*
> *and will protect and guard you from the evil one.*
> **2 Thessalonians 3:3 AMP**

Irvin and Stephanie's tardiness stretched on for an hour and fifteen minutes, a delay that seemed interminable as Peter's distress grew palpable with each passing minute. Sensing his anxiety, Lucas said a heartfelt prayer for Peter's peace. By the time Irvin and Stephanie finally arrived, a mere forty minutes remained of the allotted visitation time. Throughout the brief encounter, Peter's eyes remained fixated on us, a silent plea for reassurance that we hadn't vanished.

As the visit drew to a close, we made our way to the exit, Irvin and Stephanie trailing closely behind. Sensing Peter's lingering unease, Lucas and Abigail instinctively escorted us to our waiting car. In that moment, amidst the turmoil of the visit, I sensed a profound shift within Peter. It was as if he understood, deep in his heart, that he was safe, and that he need not return to Irvin and Stephanie's home again.

I will say of the LORD,
He is my refuge and my fortress;
my God in Him will I trust.
Psalm 91:2 KJV

This phase marked a turning point for both Peter and me. The arrival of a new mental health counselor at Peter's school brought a sense of relief, their patience and understanding coupled with a staunch commitment to confidentiality fostering a safe space for Peter's growth. As we adapted to new routines, a harmonious equilibrium emerged, offering a sense of stability that had been absent before. The relentless encounters with malevolence and deceit had left deep scars.

I continued weekly sessions with Isabella. Through her guidance, the journey toward healing unfolded, proving to be a vital lifeline in my recovery process.

After several years marked by turmoil, Peter and I experienced a rare gift of tranquility during Thanksgiving and Christmas, surrounded by the loving embrace of our newfound family in Christ. While many may count grand blessings, our hearts overflowed with gratitude for the simple joys of peace and serenity that graced our lives. For us, true abundance lay in the absence of fear and worry that once plagued Peter's weekends, no longer bound by the necessity of staying overnight in a place where safety felt elusive. In the embrace of this newfound simplicity, we found solace and contentment beyond measure.

For the first time in years, I savored the bliss of celebrating my birthday in undisturbed tranquility, relishing every moment spent with Peter, free from any distractions. As I reflect on the abundance of blessings surrounding me, I am keenly aware of the profound impact of persistent prayers, both my own and those of countless others. Through unwavering faith and a steadfast commitment to seeking justice, I witnessed the miraculous hand of God moving mountains to pave the way for this newfound life. Each hurdle overcome and every obstacle surmounted stands as a testament to the power of God's intervention, shaping a future filled with hope and promise.

Jesus looked at them and said,
"With man this is impossible,
but with God all things are possible."
Matthew 19:29 NIV

Closing Thoughts

Because this is a true story, the names of all the people involved have been changed for their safety and anonymity. In light of the events that have taken place, I am grateful to say that I am healthier and happier than I have ever been in my life. God truly has performed miracles, signs, and wonders in my life. He continues to do so as I remain close to Him through daily reading of His Word, consistent communication with Him through prayer, and very importantly, the amazing faith-filled believers He has placed in my life to love and call friends and family.

I believe wholeheartedly that if we draw near to God, even when it feels as though there is no one around, He will plead our cause and protect us. And He will send the people we need and that need us at the perfect moment. I encourage anyone experiencing anything similar to some of the challenges I have faced to always draw near to God, practice humility, admit we need help, and seek it out with God's guidance. We can help serve God through helping others who need help, giving them hope by sharing our stories with them.

Thank you so much for taking the time to read about my life. I would like to close by praying for all who have read or may read my book.

~

Dearest Heavenly Father,

LORD, I am so grateful for Your intervention in my life,
and I ask today that anyone who has read or will read this book
would be blessed by what You have done for me
and that You will meet them
where they currently are,
increasing their faith
and seeing how real You are in their lives.
Please bless their families
with prosperity and good health,
as Your Word promises in 3 John v. 2.
May Your Spirit guide them
in the season of life they are in.

In Jesus' Name.
Amen.

About Azariah Nasya

Azariah Nasya felt a strong calling from God to share her personal story of overcoming adversity as a testimony of His faithfulness. With a background marked by dysfunction yet still interwoven with God's presence and hope, she intimately understands the struggles many face. Azariah hopes to increase readers' faith by conveying that God actively provides for His children's needs when they trust in Him.

Having personally experienced addiction, abuse, depression, and more, Azariah walks with readers in their pain and most importantly, towards healing. She offers the hard-won perspective that we must make time for self-care as we replace destructive habits with healthy ones.

While this is her first book, Azariah has been writing since college. Her raw, firsthand account is unmatched in its authenticity. Through her journey's pivotal moments, like her son's second removal from her custody, Azariah learned to lean fully on God, who delivered her. She wants readers to know that despite her flaws, her enduring love for the Lord inspires her to love others each day.

∽